The Lure of the Dolphin

The Lure of the Dolphin

Robin Brown

AVON
PUBLISHERS OF BARD, CAMELOT AND DISCUS BOOKS

THE LURE OF THE DOLPHIN
is an original publication of Avon Books.
This work has never before appeared in book form.

AVON BOOKS
A division of
The Hearst Corporation
959 Eighth Avenue
New York, New York 10019

Published by arrangement with the author.
Library of Congress Catalog Card Number: 78-63603
ISBN: 0-380-43158-0

First Avon Printing, April, 1979

Printed in the U.S.A.

The Lure of the Dolphin

Foreword

by John C. Lilly, M.D.

BELIEFS about dolphins, their intellectual capacity, their humor, their way of life, are changing. The new beliefs that are supplanting the older have led to the current conflicts and controversies that exist among scientists and among lay people. *The Lure of the Dolphin* is a remarkable book in that it is written at the interface between two extreme types of belief. The first type are the classical scientific beliefs inherited from the 19th century; the second type are based upon an open-minded approach to the dolphins and experiencing them directly in their interactions with us. As Robin Brown states, "Those who have swum with dolphins somehow are changed in their beliefs about dolphins." Those who make academic judgments about dolphins without directly experiencing them foster and maintain the beliefs inherited from the time of Darwin.

The clue to these controversies can be found in the kinds of knowledge that are brought to bear upon the problem of dolphins versus humans.

In my own experience coming from a neurophysiological, neurological and psychoanalytic background, I was able to elicit from and with the dolphins, information that gave rise to a new set of beliefs epitomized in the two books, *Man and Dolphin* and *The Mind of the Dolphin.* More recently I have completed a book called *Communication Between Man and Dolphins: The Possibilities of Talking With Another Species.* The latter book summarizes our discoveries about dolphins and presses the new belief system about them to the forefront.

In the Human/Dolphin Foundation in Malibu we are busy designing, building and realizing a method of communication that will surmount the physical barriers between man and dolphin. In the new set of experiments proposed in the program called JANUS we are interfacing a computer with two JANUS faces; one facing the dolphin and operating appropriately in his set of parameters, and the other facing the human and operating appropriately in the human set of parameters. The computer will furnish the wherewithal to change from one continuum to the other. The dolphin's world is under water; the human world is in the air. By developing a code in cooperation with the dolphins, we predict that we will be able to communicate with them on a highly abstract, complex and rapid level of operation.

This book gives some of the background that led us to this program and that led others to support it by their donations to the nonprofit Human/Dolphin Foundation. To date we have raised in the order of $100,000 for the hardware and the software for this new apparatus. During the next few years in cooperation with dolphins we will perfect our methods.

Apparently there are now enough people interested in the communication program so that we can operate in this particular way. The personnel of the Human/Dolphin Foundation are all volunteers, experts in their own fields of software, hardware and fund raising.

I first became aware of Robin Brown when I saw a motion picture on public television called, "The Lure of the Dolphins." The movie did not mention my past work with dolphins and spoke only of a dichotomous division in the mind of the producer, one that was divided between the classical, biological point of view and a more holistic view of the dolphins that relied on the movie maker's experience and the experience of those whom he contacted. I was struck with a remarkable parallel of these movie makers acting out a peculiar divided state of mind in which they interviewed various European and English scientists in two ways: An official approach in which the scientists spoke as scientists from a secure scientific position and an "off-the-records" approach in which the same scientists owned up to a more emotional and involved view of the dolphins. In the movie there was a long discussion of anthropomorphism as the sin of science, that is, the projecting of human characteristics onto an animal.

Over the years I have come to another view of anthropomorphism: We are anthropos, we have the form of anthropos and we have the thinking of anthropos. Therefore, on a strictly philosophical plane, we are anthropomorphic, having the form, and we are anthropocentric, being centered in ourselves. We have spoken to no other species; we communicate only with one another and we create a consensus human reality that may or may not agree with nature as found surrounding our cultures. We are so involved in our written records, in our textbooks, in our newspapers, our TV and our radio that we as men and women speak only with and about men and women.

I am hoping that if and when we can communicate with dolphins that we leave the anthropomorphic-anthropocentric point of view behind and become educated by at least one other species and gain more of a perspective on ourselves and the universe of life on this planet.

Our brains have only been the present size for about 200,000 years. One million years ago our brains were two-thirds their present size; two million years ago they were one-third their present size.

In contrast, the dolphins and the whales first started having brains the size of our present brains about twenty-five million years ago. Since that time they have evolved very much larger brains, brains of up to 9,000 grams for the sperm whale. Therefore, they are much more ancient than we are, have been busy with an evolution in the sea quite counter to ours and have developed their own cultures and, apparently, communicate throughout the 71 percent of our planet covered by water. It is my belief that the dolphins and the whales communicate practically on a daily news basis throughout the oceans. From this cetacean gossip they probably learn a good deal about us and our relationships to the sea. They do not learn about the human consensus reality which we hug to ourselves on the dry land, but they do learn about us in terms of our oceangoing vessels, our ocean warfare, our submarines, our atomic bombs, our torpedoes, our propeller noises and the various kinds of ways that we have of killing them. If one makes the basic assumption that they are highly social, communicate on a very high level of symbolic kinds of transactions, then what we've been doing to them in our ignorance is totally reprehensible and without foundation in the facts of their existence. It is high time that we desisted from all of our killing behaviors and moved on to finding out where and how and what cetaceans think, do and feel.

This book is an education in this transition period between the sterile beliefs of the past and the more fecund ideas of the future.

These new ideas are yet to be tested fully; there is a lot of ancillary evidence that we will have success but let us do the experiments and find out.

For those who wish to know something of the history of these developments, this book can be very valuable. For those who wish to revise their beliefs this book plus *Communication Between Man and Dolphin* is the beginning education in these matters.

Acknowledgments

A great number of people have helped me find the theme of this book, which, because it is not simply a textbook about dolphins, required almost as much emotional judgment and debate as factual research and study.

For the latter I am particularly grateful to Dr. John C. Lilly and his wife, Antonietta, for allowing me access to a substantial part of their voluminous works; and to Dr. Willem Dudock van Heel, who has provided me with a place to study dolphins. For the former, I thank Heather Lowe. Anthony Grey will remember the many days of debate during which concepts were built from the raw material of dolphin fact.

And in conclusion a special note of appreciation for the insights of an enlightened naturalist, Robert Ardrey, whose books rescued me from a tangled web of dolphin information and provided clarification of purpose. This passage in particular from Ardrey's *The Territorial Imperative* describes the purpose of this book more succinctly than anything I could write:

> Were we in a position to regard our knowledge of man as adequate in our negotiation with the human circumstance and to look with satisfaction on our successful treatment of such human maladies as crime and war, racial antagonism and social loneliness, then we might embrace the world of the animals simply to enjoy its intrinsic fascinations. But I find no evidence to support such self-satisfaction. And so the wealth of information concerning animal ways, placed before us by the new biology, must be regarded as a windfall in a time of human need.

Contents

Introduction

ALL my working life I have studied, written and made documentary films about animals. For the first ten years this interest was largely centered upon the species, homo sapiens—what Desmond Morris has so aptly named The Naked Ape—or more simply, us.

In those days as a young journalist (and a young naked ape properly endowed with a sense of superiority) I was not particularly aware of the interrelationship between us and all the other animals who claim this planet as their home. But fortunately, if painfully, those years were spent in Africa, and I was able to study not only the so-called wild animals of the Serengeti, Wankie and Ngorongoro Game Parks but the naked apes protecting their territory and fighting to hold land taken from others in ways much more bestial than those of the beasts of the bush.

I wrote two political novels defending the cause of the black apes. So far as my own tribe of white apes were concerned these put me on the wrong side, and I fled to England where my knowledge of African animals found me a niche in the television media. Ten years after my departure from Africa, with some thirty documentary films under my belt, it seemed as if human animals were becoming the dominant area of interest until I discovered two extraordinary species—the human eccentric and the dolphin.

I made thirteen hours of programs about human eccentrics,

never quite sure whether I was, in fact, in contact with an extremely rare branch of the naked ape family who seemed somehow to have overcome the unpleasant traits of the rest of the species, or a completely separate branch of the animal kingdom that had more in common with the gentle, fun-loving chimpanzees of the bush than with the naked apes of the urban jungles.

When I discovered dolphins all the pieces dropped into place.

As a device for understanding dolphins, the human eccentric may seem unusual. In fact they both have one vital factor in common—the ability to engage in what the rest of us may regard as totally pointless activities in a meaningful, life-enhancing way.

It took a little time to see the connection because when I made my first contact with dolphins, my knowledge of them was of the order one can acquire from *National Geographic* articles or a visit to a dolphinarium. I knew they were mammals, not fish, and that they displayed trainability pointing to a high level of intelligence.

Then I was lucky enough to spend three months in the Azores, on Teceira Island, to make a film about an attempt to find perhaps the most famous galleon in history—Sir Francis Drake's flagship, the *Revenge.* I took a professional diving course and although we did not find the *Revenge* I made two more important personal discoveries which have had an influence on my concepts ever since. One was the new dimension of the world beneath the sea where the absence of gravity offers the weighty human torso—and the weight-oriented human brain—unique freedoms. The other was dolphins at play in a world to which they have made a sublime evolutionary adaptation.

I have yet to meet a diver who has not been "changed" by contact with dolphins, and there are several stories in this book to show the extent to which that phrase is an understatement. These alterations of perspective move through several traditional stages. At first there is an invasion of status—the dolphin is so patently more adept in the sea than the most skilled human diver. There follows an extension of respect—a realization that this "adeptness" is something more than an example of superb physical prowess. Then there occurs a growing acceptance of another intelligence, although manifestations of intelligence are more subtle since in the sea dolphins do not perform the inane tricks they are asked to practice in dolphinariums. The first indication is curiosity; animals who have at first shown wariness are inexorably drawn by their inquiring minds into closer contact.

And finally, if you are so lucky as to be around a wild dolphin long enough, the diver is suddenly, and magically, in contact. Dolphin and diver forget the barriers created by their different shapes and abilities and join in a joyful bond that bridges the species gap and, in the case of the human conditioned all his life to believe he is the only advanced intelligence, provokes a sense of discovery and wonder that covers many emotions.

This book about dolphins is written from that platform of wonder but explores in particular one broad aspect which caused me to wonder most and causes my work with human eccentrics to have relevance.

Earlier contact with human animal species had left me with no great regard for their claim to a special status in the natural kingdom. There seemed considerably more evidence to support the theories of many contemporary anthropologists and zoologists that we are still a relatively primitive evolutionary group. But in observing human eccentrics I seemed to have discovered a naked ape that was higher up the ladder than most.

As "out-of-step" as their various activities and interests might appear to a society conditioned to the famous Protestant work ethic, they all displayed compassionate natures, a highly developed sense of humor, open contempt for fixed lines of thinking and an intense interest in anything new. In most cases their interests were also their work and this seemed to be the key to their contentment. They had amalgamated play and work into a satisfying life-style.

Yet to their fellow humans living establishment lives they were somehow inferior and treated with the gentle condescension we reserve for village idiots and the mentally subnormal.

I found this paradox impossible to resolve until encountering the dolphin in his natural habitat. These animals, it slowly dawned on me, were the "eccentrics" of the sea. Only here they were the prime species! Their extensively documented sense of humor, their extraordinary bodies refined by time to a perfect adaption to the sea, their inherent curiosity in everything that moves, and above all, their life of play/work/love which may not be separated into parts, was not eccentric in the fishy world of ganglia and baseball-sized brains. They were the grand intelligence of the oceans, unquestionably the most highly evolved species.

In their world they represented a clear demarcation of the steps up the evolutionary ladder whereas in the human world the steps have become blurred among the tribes of the naked apes.

As such, dolphins have something to offer the human species which is infinitely more important than an enjoyable performance or a companionable swim. And I believe we have an instinctive understanding of that potential. Dolphins have held an inexplicable lure for man since the beginning of recorded time and there now exists the knowledge to define that Lure.

ONE

A Shared Start

MAN and dolphin have evolved hand in hand since the beginning of finite time. This is perhaps the single most important fact our species must recognize if we are to see the cetaceans, the family of sea mammals of which the dolphin is a member, in a right context.

We share our beginning with all the other life forms conceived in the cooling plasma of our planet. We have no special position at the starting gate of animal life, no unique set of evolutionary stimulants, no particular route down the path of time from which we may claim special status of type, physical development or even intellect.

The very name we have given ourselves—"primate," generally interpreted as "prime animal"—is nothing but human arrogance, especially if we give proper consideration to the animal closest to us mentally in the natural universe—the dolphin.

The fact that the dolphin is so close to us in many recognizable ways and yet reduced by man to the status of intriguing "animal" is probably the best example of that arrogance. Only a few decades ago that most knowledgeable observer of the sea, Herman Melville, in *Moby-Dick* (Appendix 1), categorically refused to accept that dolphins were not fish in spite of a wealth of information to the contrary dating back to the time of Aristotle. Even today, with dolphinariums and sea zoos attracting huge audiences in almost every land, the fact that dolphins are much closer to humans than they are to fish is generally not known.

So let us set the basic record straight at this early stage before moving on to a more important consideration—that as animals go the dolphin is a more advanced species than the animal man.

Dolphins, like us, are mammals. They have lungs and they must surface to breathe air. They have excellent eyes and sharp ears, although their ears have no flaps. Inside their superbly streamlined and, if you like, fish-shaped bodies, they have a skeleton essentially similar to ours, refined to the demands of their sea world.

Inside their flippers they have "finger bones"; at the base of the body trunk they have the vestigial remains of hip/leg bones. Dolphins can live out of water for extended periods in the same way as man can live in it for quite a long time. We get cramps in water; they get cramps out of it, because their bodies have grown used to a supportive cushion of water. Dolphins catch colds, and have stomach aches if they overeat. They get lonely and they get depressed.

The brain of the dolphin is very large and every bit as complex as ours. They are warm-blooded, and perhaps more important, warm-hearted. It is, in fact, very hard to see how anyone who has ever watched a dolphin, either in the sea where they seek out boats and swimmers, or in a dolphinarium where they respond to their trainers like quicksilver, could compare the dolphin with the deliberate and, frankly, mindless movements of fish.

In summary, dolphins are our brothers and our sisters in the sea. The only real difference is that while man has made only minor modifications to the shape of his body, and as an extension of this, his ability to use the earth space he commands, the dolphins have made huge changes and enjoy a concept of space and freedom which is beyond human comprehension.

But then the dolphin has been around in an identifiable dolphin form for a great deal longer than man has been identifiable as a man rather than an ape. Nevertheless we give ourselves the title "prime." If we compare the evolutionary history of dolphins and man there is no justification whatsoever for this title and such bias, or arrogance, is not simply a human aberration. The proverb "Pride comes before a fall" is a concise description of the collapse not just of civilizations but also of species and races, as the wars of this century have illustrated. In the interests of our own survival it is high time we faced the fact that human history is very short while that of the dolphin is very long.

The story of early life on earth is a chapter of tragedies that render ridiculous any concept that there was, is, or ever will be a prime, or, as the word implies, sublime and virtually immortal species.

For perhaps a billion years, as the fossil record shows, the earth was conquered and ruled by multifaceted, many-eyed centipedal things called trilobites. But their desperate searching for the perfect form and their extended tenure of the planet, which in human terms comes close to our concept of immortality, eventually came to nothing.

As time rolled on across the face of the earth—and we are considering a sphere that geologists can now date back some five billion years—the story of the trilobites was echoed by a kaleidoscope of life forms, organisms so varied as to make the evolutionary process seem like the games of a cosmic clown.

Bony fishes proliferated in the Cambrian epoch, and plants that were more like scaly insects moved onto the shores of Devonian lakes and were crushed by creatures resembling dragons. During the Carboniferous period the whole planet became a giant greenhouse from pole to pole and the skies filled with giant insects, only to be replaced in the Permian by virtually mindless saurians. But although the dinosaurs were to rule the earth for 100 million years they arrived, in their time, at their end.

Their apparently sudden demise contains an object lesson for man, as the astronomer Fritz Kahn has already pointed out:

> Are not two hundred million years enough for the dominance of a family, and a hundred million years for the despotism of giants? Is not Olympus vacant now and the Parthenon in ruins? Why do we

expect any stock to be immortal? Everyone knows that everything mortal is mortal. . . . Families die out, so do nations, races: and so too have the saurians disappeared.

It only seems rapid to us because it lies so far back in the past and because in a hundred million years you can toss ten million around as if it were nothing.

Humans, unfortunately, do not have the right to "toss ten million years around as if it were nothing." Our special status is based on a scant four million if you stretch the history of identifiable man to the limit of credibility.

Dolphins, on the other hand, do have that right. There were identifiable cetaceans in the seas of old earth thirty million years ago.

In the evolutionary process, or more accurately, out of the animal soup that was the sum of a swarm of evolutionary processes, dolphins arrived at a sophisticated large-brained form at least 25 million years before the descendants of man had escaped the trees.

But just as important, if we are seeking to understand the very special lure the dolphin has always had for man—a unique empathy that often overrides our traditional contempt of "lesser" species—is the fact that dolphins and man come from the same root stock. We share the successful branch of evolution that resolved itself in the modern mammals, and the mammals are unquestionably the most refined organisms ever to move on the face of the planet.

Man was to resolve his future and find his contemporary shape and mentality on the land, while the dolphin chose the sea. But both began as land mammals, and the shared ancestors of both dolphin and man may be found in the "shadow" mammals which scurried beneath the giant feet of the dinosaurs during the Jurassic epoch and the early Cretaceous period which followed.

We survived together. We survived when the dinosaurs, myriad species of marine life, a complete race of huge-toothed birds and the conquerors of the sea bottom, the ammonites, died out. As identifiable mammals we were still around at the end of the "Age of Extinction," as the Cretaceous period has been called, in time to participate in the greatest event in the history of the natural universe—the explosion of the Cenozoic period.

The paleontologist Herbert Wendt describes it: "As though Nature had pressed a switch at the end of the Cretaceous time hordes of completely different forms appeared: insects, bony fishes, birds and above all the mammals."

Some thirty orders of placental mammals, called eutherians, filled the great life gap left at the end of the Cretaceous period (Appendix 2). Each of these orders had several members, and the earth witnessed a melee of competing mammal life, as is demonstrated by the fact that of some thirty eutherian starters, only sixteen have made it through to modern times.

The two most successful orders, the primates and the cetaceans, survived by taking heavy evasive action. For the bushy-tailed, bug-eyed ancestors of man, the answer, in common with others, was to head for the trees. For the four-footed, slightly armor-plated ancestors of the dolphins, the seemingly safest place was the water.

The primal splash occurred some seventy million years ago for dolphins.

The Water's Fine!

The dolphin's first intelligent move along the road of survival, which is synonymous with evolution, is at least as old as man's, and as we follow dolphin development in the water it will become obvious that it was an infinitely more intelligent choice. For in real terms, when man-things jumped for the trees (which was no great jump at all and would have to be traumatically reversed in the distant future) the dolphin-things literally jumped into space. They left this world, a world for which their ancestors had spent eons of time perfecting them (providing them with lungs, evolving their legs, armoring their bodies), and entered an alien universe, a place in which they could no more live and breathe properly than could a man on the moon. The astronauts needed special suiting, air-breathing mechanisms and massive computers. Two of these they were able to strap upon their backs; the other item was too heavy to carry. The dolphin-things need special suiting, air-breathing mechanisms and massive computers. They built them into their bodies, and built them, in earth terms, very quickly.

As Edwin H. Colbert, Curator of Fossil Reptiles and Amphibians at the American Museum of Natural History, puts it: "Of all the mammals the whales and porpoises [dolphins] are certainly the most atypical and in many ways the most specialized in the extent to which they have developed from their primitive eutherian ancestors."

There is another, even more intriguing mystery about dolphins and their big brothers the whales. When they went into the sea it is almost as if they disguised their tracks. All our knowledge of how we and every other animal evolved is based on two main areas of scientific investigation: on rock-hard remains or impressions of forms left in rocks, called fossils, and on an elegant scientific form of jigsaw-puzzle work in which the expert will say, "This bit fits this bit," and so on.

The only trace we have ever found of a fossil cetacean (the group label for whales and dolphins) is an ancient whale that was already very much a whale even though it was different from modern whales. It was found in sediments from the Middle Eocene age of some fifty million years ago—a very early period for developed mammals, but by then it was already 60 feet long and had "built" new body structures—fins and flippers.

As an indication of the kind of evolutionary jump this animal must have made it is relevant to point out that by this time it is questionable whether the ancestors of man had got much further than lemurlike tree dwellers or at best the most primitive of gibbonlike apes. He is totally unidentifiable as man.

What is more significant, and puzzling to the scientists, is that this huge ancient whale was in a sense a factory reject. He wasn't good enough and he became extinct. He is not the ancestor of the modern cetaceans. Possibly the greatest mystery of natural history is that no missing links to the modern whales and dolphins have ever been discovered. It is as if the oceans were seeded by forces or persons unknown at a period long before man was there to watch or record, 25 million years ago. Colbert goes some way to acknowledging this mystery with a note which occurs in his listing of mammals: "The third cohort, Mutica [the sixteen orders of living mammals are scientifically grouped under four main headings called "cohorts"], contains only dolphins and whales who are quite obviously a quite separate group of mammals from early times."

The most likely explanation of this gap between the ancient whales, the Archaeoceti (Zeuglodontia), and the ancestors of the modern dolphins is that the Archaeoceti, who were full sea whales, were wiped out by some great natural disaster which did not quite obliterate another branch of the early cetacean family that lived in swamps, estuaries and rivers.

The best we can do in tracing the dolphin's ancestors from the primal splash to today is to study some of the more intriguing members of the dolphin family that live in places climatically similar to those which existed at times in the distant past.

After the Carboniferous, the early Cenozoic age (also known as the Tertiary), which began what might be called the "mammal boom," was one of the most luxuriously vegetated periods the earth had known. Trees and plants reached out again to touch the edges of the icecaps, and all that was land was green with trees and plants like laurel, magnolia, cypress, other pines and even deciduous trees and grapevine. It was a turn of the wheel similar to that which happened eons before in the Permian, when volcanic activity filled the atmosphere with carbon dioxide and resulted in the blanketing of the earth with its most comprehensive vegetable carpet.

In the rain forests and the tropical jungles of the Tertiary the dolphin ancestors almost certainly lived, and it was here they became swamp dwellers, later river dwellers. Finally these early river dolphins made their way to the sea, where they found a world rich in food, free of the mammal predators and with ample room in which to grow and develop.

Certain rare species of dolphin still exist today in tropical swamps, inland lakes and warm rivers, and it can surely be no accident that they display apparently archaic features. They are in fact living "missing links" or at least simulacra of the earliest dolphins.

Called platanistids, there are four species, each of a separate genus—the La Plata dolphin, the bouto, the susu and the Tung Ting Lake Dolphin. They are unquestionably the most intriguing of the dolphins.

The La Plata, as its name indicates, is a South American species, and although its natural home is the freshwater river it will happily enter the sea. It is thin and rarely longer than 6 feet. The feature which interests scientists looking for a link with primal ancestors is the animal's long "beak." It is such a distinctive feature, armed with more than two hundred needle-sharp teeth, that early researchers believed that they had found a living relative of a famous marine reptile, the ichthyosaur—indeed, seen from the side the La Plata looks more like an ichthyosaur than it does a modern dolphin. This impression was soon qualified, and the La Plata is in every other sense a true mammalian dolphin. The fact remains that they live in a Tertiary-type environment and the beak is unquestionably like a reptile beak.

In an even steamier jungle habitat, the Amazon basin, lives the bouto. This species also occurs in the Guianas and in the Brazilian Orinoco, and there has been much speculation among zoologists that these separate but similar species that are apparently neighbors may have developed completely independently on either side of the South American continent. There is even a theory, which would certainly justify their reputation as living dolphin fossils, that they evolved on different ancient continents and were joined by continental shift.

The bouto also has a long, toothy beak. There is a definite neck region, and its flippers are particularly interesting, being large and well spread with the "finger" bones (all dolphins have the equivalent of man's hand buried in their flippers) clearly visible. These flippers are used almost as legs when the bouto finds itself in shallow swamp water almost without room to swim. It also has short seallike bristles on its face.

In the Ganges, Brahmaputra and Indus rivers, we find a dolphin that is completely blind, although to which point of evolution this degenerate vision belongs is of great speculative interest. Did the susu once have eyes and then allow them to degenerate because, in the muddy rivers, they were of no use, or has it never bothered to develop proper eyes? The susu shares the archaic features of the other platanistids, but has an even more flexible neck and no backfin, and its blowhole is a single slit.

Finally, the exquisitely named Tung Ting Lake dolphin, a small animal shining white beneath, silvery gray-blue above, with a personality to suit its name in that it is famous for its leaps and darting play. The lake is 600 miles up the Yangtze River in China, but, for reasons no one has ever explained, the animal has never been known to swim downriver. Otherwise "normal," the Tung Ting has the platanistid's archaic beak, sometimes a foot long, and it shares the mud-happy habits of the bouto, leaving the lake at certain seasons of the year to visit shallow tributaries, and it has been seen frolicking in mud-filled pools and ditches.

There is one concluding aspect of the platanistids which would again point to an ancient status: they have a mystical, almost godlike place in the myths and legends of the people whose lands they inhabit. Jacqueline Nayman, in *Whales, Dolphin and Man*, records that in South America the bouto of the Amazon are considered sacred and must not be killed. "They are said by the Indians to have been fond of young girls and to disguise themselves as humans at carnival time. If an unmarried girl becomes pregnant it is believed that the bouto is responsible and this is not considered a disgrace."

Almost all the Polynesian islands have folk stories in which dolphins have mystical roles, and in his book *We Chose the Islands* Sir Arthur Grimble is able to present an eyewitness account of a legend coming true. On the Gilbert Islands he is told that the high chiefs of the Butaritari and Makin-Meang tribes maintain hereditary dolphin callers; these mystics make their contact while in a trance state.

Grimble actually becomes involved with one of the mystics: ". . . my faith was beginning to sag under the strain when a strangled howl burst from the dreamer's hut . . . his cumbrous body came hurtling head first through the torn screens . . . 'They come, they come, our friends from the West.' "

In company with the tribe, Grimble goes to stand in the surf and watches a school of dolphins heading swiftly for the spot, slowing as they approach the waiting men. " 'The King out of the West comes to meet me,' the dreamer murmured, pointing downward. My eyes followed his hand. There, not ten yards away, was the great shape of a dolphin poised like a glimmering shadow in the glass-green water. Behind it followed a whole dusky flotilla of them."

The eminent zoologist Ivan Sanderson does not record these legends in his *Living Mammals*, although he records an excellent example of archaic bouto behavior—"the author once encountered them in Guiana in knee-deep water among giant tree-boles then miles from the nearest river" (coincidentally an excellent description of a Tertiary swamp-forest). But when he turns to the subject of the Tung Ting dolphin, living on the other side of the earth from the Amazon, he does find a god-legend. "The Chinese fishermen never molest these animals on the grounds that it embodies the spirit of a Princess who committed suicide in the lake."

Sanderson concludes, as have the majority of zoologists, "The distribution of the platanistids is very odd and would seem to indicate that they really are leftovers from a once much more numerous and universally distributed ancient group of animals."

What then is left of the jigsaw that might fill in the gap between the first water-oriented mammals and the archaic platanistid dolphins? Bits and pieces; scraps that can be attached only at random and speculatively on this more definite fabric, like fragments on a collapsed Greek mosaic that may or may not fit. Some modern dolphins have bony plates in the skin of their backs. Some extinct dolphins had interlocking lines of bony discs, like armadillos. The giant otter, beavers, manatees and dugongs, all water-oriented mammals, have tails which could demonstrate the various steps by which dolphins evolved their singular horizontally opposed tails.

The mosaic would seem to shape up like this, and it is a film strip rather than a still picture. A four-footed mammal living ever closer to water during the Tertiary deluge; entering the warm tropical muddy environment; evolving its forelimbs into wide fins that would serve both as paddles for water and arms for humping over mudbanks; flattening and losing its neck and the flexibility of the head; keeping for a long time the food tool of its beak but sharpening and strengthening the teeth that must catch and hold swift-swimming, slippery fish; abandoning altogether its now pointless hindquarters until only hip bones remain to support the newly grown tail; finally turning from the swamp and the restrictions of the mud . . . into the deep rivers . . . into the sea!

And where is man, the primate, while all this is going on? Where is the ancestor we have placed on record as the "prime animal," because our film strip is at least forty million years long and it is time to ask the question, "Who leads in evolution?" Not in building or warring, or changing the face of the earth or for that matter the moon, because these are success values, marks of achievement, we as men have invented. They are not necessarily—arguably, not in any sense—milestones to a superior state of being.

As the dolphin changed, adapted, began moving toward what contemporary zoologists have described as the most perfectly adapted animal in the natural universe, we were clinging nervously to the trees, a round-eyed, jittery lemur. While the dolphin swims on in search of a place where he will change himself into the shape and mind of a being that deserves Utopia, we will consider the progress of man via a process which seems as "natural" to his nature as peace and tranquillity are natural in the dolphin—the method of kill and destroy.

The Leap of the Mean Monkey

The monkey that leapt from the trees toward "manliness" had to kill to eat, there is no questioning that. He was a tiny, lemurlike animal who in terms of our other example, the dolphin, took a very long time to make those first evolutionary steps to a more adept, larger-brained, upstanding form. When the ancient whale had already developed a brain large enough to manage a huge body in a totally alien environment for an air breather (the brain this requires is explored later in this book), man was still less than halfway between a lemur and a primitive monkey, and the steps he was taking were infinitely less traumatic.

Fifty million years ago, using the fossil skull Adapis found in chalk sediment near Paris as evidence, man was still a lemur. Twenty million years later, on the evidence of the Egyptian fossil find Aegyptopithecus, he was still in the trees, still a primitive ape, and now we are getting very close to the present in earth time.

In the ocean, whales and dolphins were moving much faster along the evolutionary track. They had not only climbed inside a streamlined body that still baffles modern engineers but they had stripped off excess, unwanted parts and built equipment for their new universe, like dorsal fins and an extraordinarily powerful motor, more powerful than the screw of any ship, the horizontally opposed tail.

Great excitement occurred in the '50s among prehistorians when it looked as if a fossil discovered in an Italian mine, Oreopithecus, was about to prove that the tardy ancestors of man had at least managed to put one foot across the line into "manliness" twenty million years later, or about ten million years ago—the very recent in earth time. By this time, using the Amazon ancient dolphins as our evidence, the cetaceans had large brains, excellent eyes, finely adapted bodies and even an echo system for locating objects.

As it turned out, Oreopithecus was to dash man's hopes once

again. The German biologist Gerhard Heberer was finally to report:

> It was certainly no ancestor of ours, but in all probability a sub-human anthropoid ape. . . . it proves that the hominid stock was already independent ten million years ago; it shows us also, however, that the hominids did not descend from long-armed arboreal apes of the tropical rain forests. For at that time, ten million years ago, in all probability there were not yet any long-armed anthropoid apes.

In truth, the missing link, that magical transitional apeman which man has sought so desperately out of the same kind of loneliness that makes us ache to discover life on other planets, has not yet been found. In East Africa the extraordinary Leakey family has done more than any others to identify a somewhat disjointed section of the more recent steps on the ladder, but in earth-time terms they are so recent as to be almost modern, and in any event the point is probably made. Man, the primate, is only prime by his own definition. A study of the evolution of dolphins and man marks man as the late developer.

But this book is primarily concerned with the relationship between man and dolphins, and we should not be too concerned with the simple factor of evolutionary time. In fact, *how* we developed rather than the time it took is much the more important question.

All the evidence would indicate that dolphins have enjoyed a placid command of their sea world for many millions of years. Swimming, learning, reshaping down the long ages, they have been sustained by an environment of peace that has been free of serious threat and richly endowed with an abundance of food and living space.

But this has not been so for man. Killing to avoid being killed, killing to eat, killing to expand, killing to hold on to his winnings, man has spent his two million years on the competitive arena of the land clubbing down neighbors of his own species, the land animals, the fish of the rivers, the birds of the sky—and today dolphins and their big brothers the whales.

And this aggressive assault did not stop when man no longer had real survival need of it.

Admittedly, dolphins kill—they eat fish. But they eat only the fish they need, and a modern dolphin is a more efficient machine, eating less than his primitive ancestor. Dolphins also have a killing tool—their bony "beaks"—but this has been developed for a limited defensive purpose. They can deliver a killing blow to their only real enemies, sharks, but normally the blow serves simply to discourage further attack. In fact, sharks are no longer the dolphin's prime enemy; that title must now be reserved for man. And yet in all the history of men and dolphins there has not been a single substantiated instance of a dolphin mounting any kind of serious attack on a human being.

Against this we must face the fact that modern man consumes much more food than his primitive ancestors, uses up infinitely more of the world's natural resources and seems completely incapable of putting down his killing tools even though he has discovered agriculture and developed relatively compassionate animal-protein farming methods.

The stone axes we needed for survival a million years ago should by now be totally redundant. But are they? Have we really come that far from the cave? As you read, a bullet is piercing a head somewhere in a war that at its roots will be about land and/or food. This year "ecologically aware" Americans who believe their society to be the peak of human development will allow the killing of at least seventy thousand dolphins so that they may continue to enjoy a tuna salad.

These are the activities of an extremely primitive animal species that possesses no more than a veneer of morality and ethics —or, and it is no less depressing, of an advanced and somewhat deadly species that has allowed the violence of its survival path to become ingrained in its nature.

Our *only* excuse is that we know no better, that we have no example by which we may monitor our behavior; that there is nothing else on earth that relates to man and his demands, appetites, needs. This book will attempt to show that that "uniqueness" justification is wrong in all its parts. There is another developed intelligent being on this planet that has come as far as we have, except that it started earlier and has already moved well ahead—the dolphin.

More important, we were once aware of the dolphin example, revered it, and it is high time we rediscovered that knowledge.

A Moment of Enlightenment

For almost all the time that the so-called advanced tribes of man have lived in a juxtaposition with the dolphin, we have either not seen them or have ignored them (the phenomenon of fearing them, manifested by films like *The Day of the Dolphin* and *Orca*, is an unpleasant, very recent development). But two thousand years ago there flowered in southern Europe a culture the like of which the world of man had not seen, before or since.

It was called the "Greek miracle." Seemingly out of nowhere an entire state of sensitive, thinking, art-loving, democratically governed people emerged, a phenomenon so rare and so exquisite it has left indelible traces in our architecture, language, forms of government, ethics, humanities, philosophy—an entire spectrum of material and spiritual monuments of which man can be justly proud.

It can be no coincidence that among the gods of these enlightened Greeks we find the dolphin.

Nothing in the evolution of man prior to that time had promised such a development, and nothing like it has happened since. Before the Greek miracle the tribes of man followed gods and values in which barbarity was a common denominator, and when finally the Greek cultural oasis and its short-lived Roman echo were overrun by barbarians, little was kept deliberately, although some features, architectural forms, political models and a great number of words proved to be immortal.

But if we are seeking to find a role—a proper association—for dolphin and man, the Greek miracle is important. It is not just our only precedent, it is also the only association worth studying in that it grew and flourished among a group of men and women who believed and practiced the kind of ethics and principles to which we must aspire—to which many do today.

Dolphins and the ancient Greeks built an association that encompassed almost every aspect of life—religion, art, music, philosophy, even practical zoology. The Greeks found the amalgam that we of this age must find; they revered dolphins, accorded them a spiritual and metaphysical status—but most important, they studied and understood them.

It was a brief moment when the pen was genuinely mightier than the sword; an age of scribblers, storytellers, diarists and note takers. Even realizing this it is still hard to accept that the first, extraordinarily accurate, minutely detailed zoological description of dolphins was written by Aristotle some two thousand years ago.

Aristotle's *Historia animalium* is a vast work, and he takes five volumes, excluding some passing references, to get to dolphins. Once there, however, his descriptions are living proof of how closely the Greeks must have observed and examined dolphins, even to the point of marking them for scientific investigation.

It is well worth remembering as you read Aristotle's account that probably 90 percent of the present world population still think dolphin are fish, rather than mammals. I experienced a pointed instance of this ignorance when I was directed to a shelf of books by an experienced librarian at a large London library. She informed me, quite innocently, that I would find all the books on fishes on one particular rack.

More than three hundred years before the birth of Christ, Aristotle wrote:

The Dolphin, the Whale and other Cetacea have no gills but a blowhole instead, are viviparous; so too are the pristis and the ox-fish. None of these is to be seen carrying eggs; they omit this stage, and begin with the actual fetation, which becomes articulated and gives rise to the young animal, exactly as occurs with the human species and the viviparous quadrupeds. For the most part the dolphin produces one offspring, occasionally two; the whale either two (more generally two) or one. The porpoise does as the dolphin. It resembles a small dolphin and occurs in the Black Sea, although it differs from the dolphin by being smaller in size and broader across the back; it is bluish gray in color. *Many people believe that the porpoise is a kind of dolphin.*

All animals who have a blowhole breathe in and out as they possess lungs. A dolphin has been observed, while asleep, with its snout above water, and snoring in its sleep. Both dolphin and porpoise have milk and suckle their young; and they take their young, while still small, inside them. The young dolphins grow quickly; they are grown to full size in ten years. The dolphin's gestation period is ten months. It bears its young in summer and at no other season; furthermore it actually disappears at the time of the Dog Star for about thirty days. Its offspring accompany it for a considerable time; in fact it is an animal that dotes on its children. It lives many years; some are definitely known to have lived for over twenty-five years; others for thirty by the following method. Fishermen dock the tails of some of them then let them go again; this enables them to discover how long they live.

In addition to this main, and as we shall see in a moment almost uncannily accurate, note on the cetacea, Aristotle reveals a deep fascination for the animal with recurring references in other sections of his encyclopedia.

The dolphin makes a squeak and moan when it is out of water and exposed to the air. . . . this animal possesses a voice since it has both lungs and a windpipe; but as its tongue cannot move freely, and it has no lips, it cannot utter any articulated sounds.

. . . they have no power of speech; this power is peculiar to man. The possession of its power implies the possession of a voice, but the converse is not true. All persons who are deaf from birth are dumb as well, although they can utter a sort of voice.

. . . in the sea between Cyrene and Egypt there is a fish called "louse" which dogs the dolphin.

The dolphin copulates lying side by side and the time taken by the process is neither short nor long. [!]

Later in this book, modern scientists using electronic and other tools beyond the comprehension even of a mind as inquiring as Aristotle's will demonstrate how difficult it has been to collect accurate information about the physiology of dolphins. Taking just a handful of the modern discoveries as an indication, it becomes patently obvious that Aristotle and the other ancient Greek naturalists who had no assistance other than their eyes must have engaged in extremely lengthy and detailed observation of the dolphin.

It is only very recently, for example, that scientists have established that dolphins do, as the Aristotle account reveals, sleep while swimming, in effect catnapping. Dolphins in fact rarely produce more than one offspring, and a feature which delights modern researchers is a young dolphin swimming in tight company with its mother and the strong bond of maternal affection which exists between the dolphin mother and its young. But this has been observed only by the use of modern tanks, cameras and underwater plate-glass windows. Aristotle's enlightened guess that porpoises are dolphins is, of course, accurate, but the mistaken terminology still prevails in America today. Keepers of modern dolphinariums had literally no idea at all as to the gestation period of the animals. It turns out that, on average, it is close to ten months. Similarly, when I asked a dolphinarium owner in 1977 how long dolphins lived his reply was that no one was absolutely sure because dolphins had been kept in pools only for the last twenty years or so—but he thought "twenty-five to thirty years is a good average." This man, I know, had not read Aristotle.

I have no idea whatsoever what Aristotle is referring to with his comment on the thirty-day disappearing act at the time of the Dog Star, but it could well be an oblique description of dolphin groups engaging in regular migrations, for which there is modern evidence. The Aristotelian description of the dolphin's vocal apparatus and its limitations is not only accurate but could almost have been lifted verbatim from dozens of modern reports by scientists who have investigated the intriguing possibility of dolphins talking.

Dolphins do suffer from infestation by the "louse"; some modern zoologists believe it to be the reason they leap about so much.

More Than Animals

In any event, even though Aristotle's account reads like a specialized textbook, he was in fact merely reflecting an interest common to his age. The interest was so intense that most popular diarists of the age included "wondrous" dolphin stories in their books. Clio, the poet Bianor, Aesop, Oppian, Herodotus, Aelian, Euhemerus, Lucian, Plutarch and in particular Pliny the Younger detailed the exploits of the intriguing animals. A mixture of gossip, fable and naturalistic observation, most of these accounts dealt directly with what the Greeks obviously thought was a very natural situation—that dolphins and man had a natural empathy, an association that was remarkable for its affection. In particular they mentioned what was obviously a quite common event which has carried through in song and fable to the present—boys on dolphins.

One of the most detailed reports is contained in Pliny's *Natural History*, and even allowing for a degree of literary licence, and the fact that Pliny is not half as good a zoologist as Aristotle, it is a very moving story and further evidence of the very special place the dolphin had for the ancient Greeks and Romans. The key passage is:

In the reign of the late lamented Augustus a dolphin that had been brought into the Lucrine Lake fell marvellously in love with a certain boy, a poor man's son, who used to go from the Baiae district to school at Pozzuoli, because fairly often the lad, when loitering about the place at noon, called him to him by the name of Snubnose and coaxed him with bits of bread he had with him for the journey,—I should be ashamed to tell the story were it not that it had been written about by Maecenas and Fabianus and Flavius Alfius and many others—and when the boy called it at whatever time of day, although it was concealed in hiding, it used to fly to him out of the depths, eat out of his hand and let him mount on its back, sheathing, as it were, the prickles of its fin, and used to carry him when mounted right across the bay to Pozzuoli to school, bringing him back in similar manner for several years, until the boy died of disease, and then it used to keep coming sorrowfully and like a mourner to the customary place, and itself also expired, quite undoubtedly from longing. [Appendix 3]

The essence of this story has considerable support in contemporary dolphin research. The American scientist Dr. John Lilly, who must be regarded as the father of modern dolphin research, certainly found evidence of love between at least one of his assistants and a dolphin called Peter during several years of work in the Virgin Islands. There is a strong suspicion among the most clinical of modern scientists that dolphins suffer acute depression if deprived of human companionship, to the point of committing suicide by "pining away." And in almost every part of the world there are well-documented recent accounts of dolphins striking up friendship, frequently and regularly repeated, with swimmers or people living by the sea. An actual case of this is being carefully studied at this moment of writing by an inhabitant of the seaside town of Bournemouth in the murky English Channel. But again it would seem that such incidents, which today we find fascinating, were, if anything, commonplace to the Greeks and Romans, as Pliny tells:

Another dolphin in recent years at Hippo Diarrhytus on the coast of Africa similarly used to feed out of people's hands and allow itself to be stroked, and play with swimmers and carry them on its back. The Governor of Africa, Flavianus, smeared it all over with perfume, and the novelty of the scent apparently put it to sleep; it floated lifelessly about, holding aloof from human intercourse for some months as if it had been driven away by insult; but afterwards it returned and was an object of wonder as before. [Appendix 4]

Pliny then turns to a story which is particularly interesting in that it could be told of dolphins which associate with primitive tribes of this century. Both the La Plata and Tung Ting Lake dolphins have a special relationship with the natives of their habitat because they help them to catch fish by driving the fish into nets.

In the region of Nismes in the province of Narbonne there is a *marsh* named Latera where dolphins catch fish in partnership with human fishermen. . . . When the entire population from the shore shouts as loud as it can, calling for "Snubnose" for the denouement of the show, the dolphins quickly hear their wishes if a northerly breeze carries the shout out to sea. Their line of battle comes into view, and at once deploys in the place where they are to join battle; they bar the passage on the side of the sea and drive the scared mullet into the shallows.

Then the fishermen put their nets around them and lift them out of the water with forks. None the less, the pace of some mullets leaps over the obstacles; but these are caught by the dolphins, which are satisfied for the time being with merely having killed them, postponing a meal until victory is won.

The action is hotly contested and the dolphins, pressing on with great bravery, are delighted to be caught in the nets, and for fear that this in itself may hasten the enemy's flight, they glide out between the nets or swimming fishermen so gradually as not to open ways of escape; none of them try to get away by leaping out of the water, which otherwise they are very fond of doing, unless the nets are put below them.

When in this way the catch has been completed, they tear in pieces the fish that they have killed. But as they are aware that they have had too strenuous a task for only a single day's pay they wait there until the following day and are given a feed of bread mash dipped in wine, in addition to the fish. [Appendix 5]

Apart from the marvelously descriptive nature of this account —literally a dolphin–man festival with everyone celebrating with a few drinks at the end of it all—what is particularly significant is the way Pliny talks about the dolphin. He appears to assume, totally naturally, that dolphins have good brains, judgment, sense and interest in what man is doing, a selfless approach to the job and a huge sense of fun. If contemporary man could only acquire this attitude we might well achieve a second miracle. We have infinitely better tools of communication and the dolphin is capable of opening his universe to us. We cannot even start along that road if we maintain an arrogant, and by definition blind, attitude to this prime species.

For the Greeks it was much more simple. Aristotle, in Greek terms, is a dry dog on the subject of dolphins, and even Pliny, although allowing the imagination freer reign, must still be seen as part clinical naturalist. But they were writing against a much more exotic background, because the majority of Greeks did not just admire dolphins, they *worshipped* them as gods.

Deities from the Sea

I went to Greece in the summer of 1977 in the interests of this book but with very few notes and no particular research schedule. This seemingly amateur approach was dictated by instinct. As I have noted in the dedication, the motive behind my several years of accumulating random bits of information about dolphins had not only eluded me to the point of frustration and irritation (a working writer can rarely afford to clutter his limited memory banks with useless information), but the whole exercise had patently gone well beyond what could be termed a normal interest in a particular animal, no matter how intriguing the beast.

I had also grown increasingly aware while talking to dolphin experts, trainers, zoologists, and a great number of natural scientists that there was, throughout, a jarring note of "wrongness" about the way people think about dolphins. It seemed to fall into two distinct categories: first, an overemotional, anthropomorphic (man with an animal shape) view; second, a cold, proof-oriented, scientific approach which seemed totally self-defeating with an animal as complex and as little understood as the dolphin.

This is all a rather complicated way of saying that I went to Greece, and in particular to Delphi, the shrine of dolphins, in search of a "muse." But extraordinarily it was in Delphi, revered by Greeks for thousands of years as the focal point (*delphys*—the navel) of the universe, that I found what I was looking for. Not from some ancient classical tome, but from a book written a few years ago by an American poet-anthropologist, Robert Ardrey!

The particular quotation which acted as the catalyst for all my doubts about motivation comes early in Ardrey's brilliant *The Territorial Imperative*, and although I have recorded it with thanks in my acknowledgments, I would propose to repeat it here because this is where it fits—in the world of Greeks and dolphins and gods, even though it is a contemporary thought.

Were we in a position to regard our knowledge of man as adequate in our negotiations with the human circumstance and to look with satisfaction on our successful treatment of such human maladies as crime and war, racial antagonism and social loneliness, then we might embrace the world of the animal simply to enjoy its intrinsic fascinations. But I find no evidence to support such self-satisfaction. And so the wealth of information concerning animal ways, placed before us by the new biology, must be regarded as a windfall in a time of human need.

I suggest that this is the only way to look at animals, whether you are a scientist or a layman. And that if there is a point, an expanded spiritual motive for looking at animals as Ardrey has so succinctly identified, the ideal animal so to observe is the dolphin. Most of this book, a description of the dolphin in all his multifaceted parts, will be devoted to justifying that suggestion.

What is more to the point here is my belief that the ancient Greeks, suspended momentarily in what, for the human race, was a brief bubble of awareness, had recognized this truth and made room for it in their theology.

But as we live in a godless age, or more particularly in an age when our gods have been trapped to the point of disbelief in a web of antiquated dogma, it is worth examining what the Greeks meant when they spoke of gods.

They were living, active, fallible, bad-tempered, sexually deranged giants, or, more simply, enlarged men and women. They were revered not for these attributes but for gargantuan status and superhuman powers which gave them the ability to protect certain sacred things. The Greeks worshipped them for their ability to look after the things that were good, things like art and music and philosophy (and wine) that were vital to the psyche of man and needed a giant to protect them. When Poseidon, whose area of responsibility was the food source of the sea, elevated a dolphin to be a god in the heavens and named for it the constellation that carries its name to this day, he deified the dolphin for kindliness, gentleness and a characteristic that should be common to all human beings, but is seemingly almost impossible for us to achieve. As Plutarch described it: "To the Dolphin alone, beyond all others, Nature has given what the best philosophers seek, *friendship for no advantage*; yet it is the friend to all men and has often given them great aid."

Sainthood Earned

The dolphin did not achieve his status with the Greeks simply from their sense of wonder, but by dint of extended example. The writings of expert naturalists like Aristotle were in their time Ardrey's "wealth of information concerning animal ways," and they were taken up by the Greeks, as Ardrey suggests we should take such information today, "as a windfall in a time of human need."

The myths and legends of the Greeks and the Romans are littered with descriptions of dolphins extending to man "friendship for no advantage."

Let us go back to Delphi. It is easy to see why this divine place (and you may interpret the word literally or figuratively) earned the title "navel of the earth." Backed by a raw mountain wall several thousand feet above a valley into which the silver olive trees flow like an extension of the sea some 20 miles away, this natural arena makes concepts of giants and their playgrounds believable.

It is the oldest and most sacred Greek shrine, although today the battered marble columns, amphitheater, ruined temples and decayed gymnasium stand more as a monument to the barbarians who overran Greece than to the splendor of its builders. Its rise to fame stems mainly from the utterances of the Delphic Oracle, the most influential group of practical prophets in history, and there is a nice pointer to human fallibility in its fall from grace. The uncannily prescient utterances of the ladies of Delphi caused it to become a necessary reference for kings and politicians for many centuries. The girls lost this enviable and profitable reputation, and Delphi began to be battered, when the word got around that they had been bribed by the Persians to give out frankly negative forecasts of the Greek chance.

But this all happened progressively as the Greek civilization decayed. In its beginning and earliest heyday, Delphi was the center of wisdom, culture, wealth and influence, thanks, according to the legends, to the various mighty gods who had their shrines there, and thanks in particular to the mighty god Apollo, protector of prophecy, divination, the arts, and music. The Muses were directly subordinate to him. But thanks most of all to the dolphin, for when Apollo founded Delphi he was endowed not with the shape of a man but with that of a dolphin.

The legend tells it as follows. Born the son of the dreadful Zeus and the Titaness Leto, Apollo (as might be expected from so tumultuous a union) grew to maturity on a heady diet of nectar and ambrosia in the remarkably short time of four days.

Impatient for kingdoms of his own, this fledgling giant left his native Delos and after visiting various likely sites for his shrine, spotted a boat in the sea off the coast near Delphi, whereupon he changed himself into the shape of a giant dolphin and leaped aboard. All proceeded to the spot known as the "navel of the earth" where Delphinius Apollo put paid to one of the more revolting of Greek religious fantasies, a snake goddess, Python, who already had something of a reputation for telling the future. In her place, Apollo the dolphin installed his own soothsayer, the first Pythia, Phenomoe, and although Apollo had to spend several years in a nearby reserve for delinquent deities as punishment for killing the Python, the place was his from then on. Protected by the dolphin god, the Pythia and her descendants proceeded to delve into the future, seated, extraordinarily uncomfortably, on a tripod over a crack in the rock that gave off intoxicating fumes, while she chewed hallucinatory laurel leaves.

But to return this to a more serious line, the dolphin from the time of Apollo on appears to have engaged in an extended campaign of good example and helping out—"for no reward," or none, at least, that was deliberately sought.

The two most classic myths which support this concern the

gods Poseidon and Dionysus. In the case of the god of the sea, a dolphin was employed for his diplomatic talents to persuade Amphitrite to become Poseidon's wife. This required all the dolphin's friendliness and goodwill, as Amphitrite had tried to escape the marriage, seeking sanctuary with a mighty protector, Atlas. For his good service the dolphin was canonized and set in the firmament as the Dolphin constellation, and there his act of disinterested friendship is immortalized to this day.

Dionysus, god of wine, used the dolphin as an object lesson. Kidnapped by Tyrrhenian pirates who sought to put him to death, Dionysus turned himself into a lion and the ship's oars into serpents and caused ivy to grow all over the ship. As gods (Apollo as an example) could suffer extended internment for murder, Dionysus turned the pirates into dolphins as the best reforming influence he could think of.

But enough of myth. The point of all this is to illustrate that the Greeks actually held dolphins above, and in a sense apart from, gods. The gods were analogies of human frailty, as a result of which they were endlessly at war. The dolphin, who was *with* the gods (and became a kind of god), was eternally helpful, generous, undemanding.

The Greeks offered the dolphin, in myth and legend, *not as a God, but as an excellent example.* That is surely how our century could afford to regard them, although I sincerely hope that any reader who might be excessively given to easy reverence of new objects and instant cults (and there are far too many of these in modern America) will carefully note the difference.

The Dolphin Analogy

The Greeks, I believe, were instinctively aware of this difference. Their religious myths, as are many of the legends of the Bible, are allegorical. As these stories evolved in ancient times they acquired the essential dramatic form that all good propaganda possesses—the need for a villain and a hero. I can think of no other explanation for the fact that throughout several centuries of writing, there is no exchange of roles—the dolphin is never the villain and, by abstract definition, it is the true symbol of god-ness (or goodness) presented and pointed up by the existence of villains all around them. Those villains were men, or men-shaped gods, and this is the subliminal message concerning dolphins in Greek literature.

Where did this message come from? Much has been written speculatively about racial memory, more of behavior dictated by instinct and more still in recent years of ethology, the precise study of innate behavior patterns in animals. But as the distinguished neurologist T. H. Bullock sums all this up: "At the bottom we do not have a decent inkling of the neuronal mechanism of learning or the physiological substratum of instinctive patterns."

At the bottom I think the Greeks had this instinctive "inkling" of the place and point in the spectrum of nature of dolphins, and their myths and legends were an attempt to entrench it. There are several pointers to the validity of this concept in ancient writings.

The poet Oppian includes this verse in his *Halieutica* (the translation is William Diaper's):

> So Dolphins teem, whom subject, Fish revere
> And show the smiling Seas their Infant-Heir,
> All other Kinds, whom Parent-Seas confine,
> Dolphins excel, that Race is all Divine.
> *Dolphins were men (Tradition holds the Tale)*
> [my italics]
> Laborious swains bred on the Tuscan Vale;
> Transformed by Bacchus, and by Neptune loved,
> They all the pleasures of the deep improved.
> When new-made fish the God's command obeyed,
> Plunged in the Waves and untried Fins displayed,
> No further charge relenting Bacchus wrought,
> Nor have the Dolphins all the men forgot;
> The Conscious Soul retains her former thought.

Now much of this is quite obviously based on the myth of Dionysus and the pirates, but how much? And in any event how much of that older tale is in itself an allegorical racially remembered version of the branching of the way for man and dolphins when the two mammals waved goodbye and went off to explore other worlds? Certainly poets of all human thinkers have special prescience. When Eliot proposes to "show you fear in a handful of dust" or Virginia Woolf moves to the edge of madness in search of the stream of consciousness (haunted by a sea creature that is very dolphinlike), they enter a territory of the mind that may be dark and inexplicable, but is unquestionably beyond the surface planes in which most of us take the time to think.

It is at least possible that there lurks in the subliminal an awareness of the joint beginnings of dolphins and man, and that the Greek poets and philosophers being less subject to racial fears or territorial imperatives were able to offer the dolphin his equal place and to accord him credit for a higher state of spiritual evolution—this recorded in their legends and myths?

If any final proof is needed I think it is to be found in an ancient Greek law which so far as I know has no equal. The more enlightened nations of our century have begun to recognize the extinction threat to many animals and have passed laws protecting them. The Greeks went one huge step further, a step which neatly rounds off their attitude to dolphins: the penalty for murdering a dolphin was the same as for the murder of a man.

The Fall

The Greeks were much given to tragedy, so it is somewhat fitting that this chapter end with one. As the Greek civilization died, so did man's first real period of empathy with dolphins.

We moved on through several centuries of dark ages, and the dolphin was lost to view. The best that can be said is that the womb of the sea which had protected them from the various excesses of the land continued to offer its timeless sanctuary.

As we approached our present time, science acquired the early shape of its present form, but it was a clinical, prooforientated exercise, excited by apparatus, tools and mathematics. A science interlocked with the humanities such as the Greeks practiced was regarded as unscientific, and concepts like equality for man and a marine beast were ridiculed and openly derided. And so it remained almost to the present day in spite of Darwin and his colleagues, who were able to face most of the truths of the natural kingdom. This comment by Norman Douglas, who has a reputation both as a biologist and a sophisticated writer, is typical. It was contained in his *Birds and Beasts of the Greek Anthology* and reviews delphic mythology.

From these and many other sources, we may gather that there is supposed to exist an obscure but powerful bond of affection between this animal and humanity, and that it was endowed with a certain kind-heartedness and man-loving propensity. This is obviously not the case, the dolphin cares no more about us than cares the haddock.

What is the origin of this belief? I conjecture that the beast was credited with these social sentiments out of what may be called poetic reciprocation. Mankind, loving the merry gambols and other endearing characteristics of the dolphin, which has a playful trick of escorting vessels for its own amusement, whose presence signified fair weather, and whose parental attachment to its offspring won their esteem—quite apart from its fabled, perhaps real, love of music or at least of noisy sounds—were pleased to invest it with feelings akin to its own. They were fond of the dolphin, what more natural and becoming than that the dolphin should be fond of them.

I will leave comment on that to Dr. Ashley Montagu, who knows infinitely more about dolphins than does Mr. Douglas: "Douglas was undisillusionedly wrong, and the dolphins are right, and so is the 'mankind' that believed in their friendliness."

Unhappily for Douglas—and he was far from being alone in his outright rejection of the "romantic" approach—our century was to see an unexpected dolphin revival.

Man, eternally in search of distraction and entertainment, recognized that the dolphin was at least more trainable than the haddock and even when trapped in pools that would put the worst forms of human penal confinement to shame would perform amazing tricks—tricks that audiences would pay large sums to see.

In a matter of years, after nearly twenty centuries of oblivion, hundreds of "Flippers" were leaping inanely, but with the dolphin's traditional, and seemingly eternal, goodwill, in marine circuses called dolphinariums, all over the world.

TWO

Meeting Again

QUITE a large number of the animals which once walked the face of our earth would be extinct now were it not for zoos.

And that, literally, is the only justification I can find for zoos. The case for dolphinariums is different, because as this chapter will show the dolphin is a long way from extinction, although the practices by which they might be pushed down that road do exist and must be carefully watched.

There was, in fact, no ecological justification for dolphinariums—for trapping dolphins in inadequate pools—when the business began in the early '30s. It was simply a business, a device for making money, and the little consideration given the dolphins was motivated by economics—keep them well and you keep them working.

The commercial cynicism of the first dolphinariums is well illustrated by their choice of a particular animal—the bottle-nosed dolphin—as a performer. They were chosen because they smiled!

In fact the bottle-nosed dolphin, or to give him his proper name, *Tursiops truncatus,* does not smile at all. The curved, somewhat knowing, slightly cynical line of the mouth is a genetic trait, and to see it as anything else is bizarre, because their mouths hold that same line when they are dying!

Commercial dolphinarium operators recognized that this fixed genetic "grin" happened to echo the facial expression humans make when they are feeling happy, and more important, friendly. Leaping, 300-pound powerhouses with a fine set of very sharp teeth don't bother us even when they are in action only a few feet away because we are crazy enough to believe that they are doing it with a friendly smile!

Recently another much larger species of dolphin, *Orcinus orca*, has appeared in the marine circuses. He has all the traditional dolphin traits of friendliness, willing cooperation and humor and is prepared, like all dolphins, to engage in idiotic commercial exercises such as opening his mouth to allow the trainer to insert his head.

But orcas don't have built-in smiles. They have big black heads and even bigger teeth, and we of the English-speaking world call them killer whales! Their commercial appeal is that of a fear-provoking monster, a King Kong of the deep.

Fortunately not all the crowds that packed the dolphinariums to thrill or quake were children and bored adults filling in a vacation afternoon. As the sea circuses boomed, the value of the stars went up and a new breed of dolphin doctors had to be found. Happily a lot of these men were scientists, and they were not fooled by the dolphin's fixed grins.

When they began, dolphinariums, a classic case of human exploitation of another species, slowly began to take on some of the justifications of decent zoos. The men who came to treat the dolphins, and the more intelligent trainers, realized they were dealing with something much larger than a circus animal. As a start, dolphins turned out to be very simple to train, infinitely easier than any circus animal we had come across before, and this included animals like dogs with long experience of human beings.

In the beginning, all the training was done by traditional methods. A trick, say the retrieval of a rubber ring, would be broken down to a simple series—the dolphin first being induced to hold the ring in its mouth, to return the ring to the trainer, to pick up the ring when placed near it, to progressively bring the ring back, and so on. The incentive was normally a food reward. Because dolphins learned so quickly—a simple trick of this kind often taking no more than an hour to perfect—few trainers indulged in punishment or pain conditioning as is used with a lot of circus animals.

As more dolphinariums opened and trainers became more experienced it began to be recognized that the science of dolphin training had special problems that made it a science apart from the conditioning of circus animals. A number of trainers discovered that food rewards were not always the best incentive—often affection and physical contact, literally a stroke and a tickle, worked better. Slow-learning dolphins were very often not slow at all—they were simply bored. Dolphins commonly picked up the basis of a trick long before a trainer recognized it and would then frustrate the trainer by injecting flourishes of their own—tossing the ring in the air and catching it, swimming round the pool with it, etc.

These gaps in understanding were not the fault of the early trainers. They were not to know that within twenty years the dolphins they were asking to find and retrieve a weighted object from the bottom of small dolphinarium pools would be working free in the open sea with radio packs strapped behind their fins; diving to huge depths to locate some of the most expensive hardware ever lost by humans.

But a few recognized the potential, and at the hands of these enlightened trainers a great breakthrough in dolphin "training" was achieved. These trainers learned not to patronize their charges. Instead of a rigid teaching program they carefully observed the dolphin's natural gymnastic ability and encouraged it.

The amazing spectacle of leaping, twisting, balancing—even "singing"—dolphins that is common fare in any dolphinarium today is a product of trainers' encouragement of dolphins to "do their own thing." Almost the only training involved is getting the dolphins to perform their stunts to a commercial sequence.

Once a trick was learned it was never forgotten, and trainers began to speculate about the dolphin's memory. In fact, the dolphins provoked questions much faster than these men could provide answers, and instead of just looking *after* the dolphinarium animals the experts began to look *at* them—with ever-increasing amazement and interest.

So by the beginning of the '50s, thanks to the dolphinariums, the dolphin had renewed his age-old relationship with man, had started to reassert the lure that he had exercised over the ancient Greeks, and the sea circuses became as important for scientific research as they were for entertainment.

At first this interest was a product of confusion. Dolphin trainers, who, it must be remembered, were a totally new breed, began to realize that things were happening outside their comprehension.

A typical case was the experiences of Christine Bowker, a young woman who went to work at Britain's first dolphinarium, at Morecambe, and found that she was falling in love (literally) with her charges and eventually—and it frightened her—that they were reading her mind.

"They were always one up on me . . . for example I was trying to get two dolphins to jump either side of me at the same time and I was actually thinking—how am I going to tell them, or indicate to them, something as complicated as that—when, literally while I was thinking it, they both did exactly what I wanted and then went whizzing round the pool making those funny chuckling noises which they make when they are pleased with themselves. It was frightening and uncanny, it bothered me so much I had to get out. Then as I sat and watched them, they did it again."

Did she believe in telepathy? "I don't even know how you classify telepathy, but they definitely knew what I wanted them to do before I actually said it."

She was even more confused by a strong but totally inexplicable feeling that she had become enclosed in some "field" of ambience. "Once you get in close contact with a dolphin you get a great big hollow inside you that can somehow never be filled. It was as if I was being haunted—and it wouldn't let go!"

Christine even made an attempt to analyze this feeling, relating it to her emotional feelings toward men. "It was very like two people falling in love . . . you know how it is, if you spot someone you like, something tingles in you. The chances are the man will notice you more, say, than the girl next to you. It felt something like that."

An extraordinary extension of this story (and I would urge my more phlegmatic readers to stay with me for a while because this is far from being an isolated case) was that Christine Bowker's "tinglings," "hauntings" or "deep hollow" (and these terms are no more abstract than those used by clinical scientists who study the paranormal) went on after she had left the Morecambe dolphinarium.

She went to live in Jersey, in the Channel Islands, where swimming is a popular sport: "It sounds crazy but when I go swimming in the sea half my mind seems to go out and I am always aware that there are dolphins in the sea."

Perhaps this young woman's reactions are hyperthyroid or purely sensual (and I know of two actual sexual experiences between dolphins and scientific researchers); the fact remains that an image was grafted on her mind, a nonscientific mind, that is stamped there indelibly to this day. And it is a very interesting message, totally alien to the strictly commercial job she was hired to do in the dolphinarium. Ask her directly the complex question of where dolphins fit in the natural kingdom (I will take a complete book to cover the same point inadequately) and Miss Bowker answers quickly and simply: "They are the next logical step to something. I don't know quite how it works out, whether they are instinctively coming towards us or we are instinctively going towards them, but I am pretty sure that if we are right with them we will get the maximum."

This, I realize, is dangerous ground, the kind that the scientist veers away from more rapidly than he would a minefield. Only for one reason, however—that it is unprovable. But one of the purposes of this book is to suggest that the dolphin is infinitely more complicated than we have dared acknowledge, particularly when it comes to his brain and his mind. Even more when the possibility exists that we may well be dealing with something that is an amalgam of mind, perfect body and freedom. And some of this is provable. The middle section of this account will deal with the work of the proof hunters—extraordinary work with extraordinary findings—but all of it in the end raising more questions than answers.

There is some proof also to be found in our limited experience of meditation, isolation and the fringe areas of the paranormal. Twenty years ago, telepathy, in fact the whole arena of "mind over matter," was a minefield as repugnant to clinical scientists as a psychic dolphin is to them today. A few had the courage to at least consider that the paranormal might exist, in particular the dedicated workers at Duke University. We now know that mind power can manifest itself physically. We don't know how, why or what, but we do know an abstract "it" exists.

To get a second opinion on Miss Bowker's objectivity I went back to Morecambe, where the training had been taken over by a husband-and-wife team of great sincerity, Steve and Shirley Gallagher. Now, I don't know whether this particular pool is peculiarly haunted, or possesses some particular psychic mirror mechanism, but it is surely an impossible coincidence that a new group of Morecambe dolphins were up to old tricks.

These tricks so disturbed the Gallaghers that they called in a research student from the psychology department of the University of Leeds. Andrew Locke's finding will be considered in detail later, but the phenomenon which resulted in his going to Morecambe belongs here.

"It began," Shirley explained, and her irritation was poorly disguised, "With them taking over the show. I would be down in our front announcement booth, well away from the show, where there is no way the dolphins can see me, and I would do my announcement: 'Good afternoon, ladies and gentlemen, the dolphin show is just about to start. . . .'

"And that's as far as I'd get! Away they went, leaping about, doing all the tricks before we could get down there. Imagine how that made us look—we were supposed to be the trainers."

I suggested that perhaps the dolphins were simply responding to the sound of the public-address announcement.

Shirley shook her head gloomily. "Oh no they weren't. I'd

also announce, using the same system, that the sea-lion show was about to start. They just ignored that and went on swimming about."

I didn't need to ask the obvious question. "Right." Shirley nodded. "They're learning English."

In fact it went further than that. The dolphins had invented their own language for Stuart: "When they want to attract my attention they go around the pool making this peculiar quacking noise which is unlike any noise they would use in the wild."

Watching the Gallaghers at work with their dolphins, one sees clearly that they have a very happy and friendly relationship. There are two pools adjoining at Morecambe, and I once saw Stuart make the mistake of turning his back while walking between the pools—with the result that a leaping funster grabbed the opportunity to nudge him head-first into the other pool.

And it's not a question of slack discipline—well, not quite. Stuart made the interesting discovery that his dolphins would respond to his commands and perform a show to the sequence he wanted rather more enthusiastically if he rewarded them with affection—smiles, claps and a tickle—instead of a bucket of their favorite fish.

"It really comes down to this," Stuart confessed. "Most of the tricks we do in our show have originally been invented by the dolphins themselves. We just exaggerate upon that particular trick and introduce a signal for it to happen in the show."

And (here it comes again), "I spent ages trying to train our most intelligent animal, Rocky, to do a particular trick, a very complicated spiral leap—and I got absolutely nowhere. The following morning I came down to the pool and was looking at him, trying to figure out a way of getting it across, when suddenly he's out of the water doing perfect twists all around the pool." Stuart thought about this for a moment, then added, "They do things every day which I think, How on earth can they figure that out?"

And then he blurted a line which seemed almost an echo of Miss Bowker's feelings of joining and contact (she, by the way, had never met Stuart and Shirley). "They come from a totally different environment from what we're used to. But I regard them as equals. I don't consider myself more intelligent just because I'm putting them through the routine, because a lot of the time it's the opposite way around—*they're making me do what they went me to do.*"

This admission seemed to give Shirley the courage to admit her own inner thoughts, and I think it's worth remembering that Andrew Locke, from the university complete with notebook and video-recording equipment, was at Morecambe when this conversation was recorded:

"I can't pin it down," Shirley explained in a rather nervous way. "I suppose people might think I'm mad, but I talk to them. Like a human being, really. I mean I know a lot of people think that's silly—they're only animals—but I do feel they think everything, you know. I mean, I feel for them . . . you know, sometimes they do appear to read your mind. There's something there, yes, there's something there; we're not just cut off completely, you know . . . there is something there between us. But I don't really know what it is . . . I don't know whether I'd like to say they could read my mind or not; I just don't know."

The truth of the matter is that Shirley Gallagher is not alone in her confusion. This gray area of uncertainty is shared at all levels of dolphin research. Unfortunately few observers, in particular members of the scientific establishment, are prepared to voice their doubts so openly, which is unfortunate, because I think we must soon start accepting that there are "possibilities" with dolphins which are outside the normal terms of scientific reference. If we do no more than total up all the unexplained features of dolphin behavior, reaction and pure question mark, I believe we would arrive at a body of evidence well worth investigating.

On that note, I want to recount a personal experience which puts me, if you wish, up there with the confused and undecided. I have experienced my own bizarre "tingle" which I cannot explain but which it would be totally dishonest, having exposed these others to question, not to recount.

It happened at the dolphinarium in Harderwijk and involved a close friend, Heather Lowe, who had accompanied me on a film trip there. While I was away on my film business, Heather had spent the morning by the pool playing catch with a dolphin, using an orange soccer ball. As I rejoined her I "saw" a ball fly from the dolphin pool (I did not see the dolphin flick it), saw her catch it and put it down. I made some comment about her doing tricks with dolphins and she, puzzled, replied, "What trick?"

Heather "believes" she did not catch the ball. It was lying beside her and had been there for some time; she had quit the game some time before I arrived. Now, I have never seen a ghost in my life, but I do have a very good memory from my filming experience of the things I do see, of shots and sequences which need to be recalled months after they have been taken. And I will swear I saw that ball move through the air and her catch it. I'll admit that the possibilities are endless—that the ball was there and I instantly associated it with its most likely game. Maybe. I think I saw it fly and I think someday someone may well prove that somebody or something fed me an action replay of an enjoyable experience.

Enough. Let us turn back from the hypothetical to the factual, with the promise that it will be no less intriguing.

The dolphin boom provoked a quantum leap in public interest in dolphins, a demand for information from people whose knowledge of the animal was limited to a brief silver glimpse of a "fish" that obviously had incredible abilities. There was a proliferation of books on the subject, even a few which took their data from ancient Aristotle but did not have the courage to admit the source. These writers had some excuse—his writings were literally the only detailed descriptions in existence at the time. Much more detailed work existed on whales, which are really large dolphins (or dolphins are small whales), because while dolphins had been largely left to swim in peace during the centuries since the ancient Greeks, whales had not. But while whales are of the same order—Cetacea (Aristotle's word)—as dolphins, the enormous difference in size puts the two mammals into totally different groups so far as the human imagination is concerned.

There was a scramble to acquire information on this "new" phenomenon, the dolphin. Old files were dusted off and reviewed, and new research programs sprang up in every country that had money to spend on research. Only a small part of this was innocent journalism to service a new public interest; the rest was pragmatic man on the make again. Right at the beginning of the dolphin craze keen-eyed representatives of government bureaucracies had spotted that this slick fish had a few secrets tucked away inside his streamlined body that man, particularly military man, who had a lot of firepower moving somewhat inefficiently on and under the sea, could use.

And so a new knowledge of dolphins was compiled. The researchers had at their disposal tools, recording devices and transport that the ancient Greeks could not have dreamed of. Admittedly "understanding" of dolphins was not added to, but "information" piled in at such a rate as to make the old information . . . well, old!

We discovered the existence of about *fifty* different species of dolphins. I apologize for that imprecise statistic but because new species are still being found and old species differentiated, it is as close as one can get.

This is not the place to list the entire order (see Appendix 6), but we will consider the broad family and then take a closer look at its main members.

There are two main types of cetaceans, and they can be differentiated by their mouths. The suborder Odontoceti have teeth. The suborder Mysticeti have whalebone (baleen) filters, and they live on shrimplike creatures called krill. We will leave the Mysticeti to swim by—they are generally regarded as the less-successful evolutionary type and there are not very many of them left anyway. I am so nervous about what is happening to whales that I'm afraid that even the mention of their name might stir the finger of some harpooner somewhere.

We will move on to the better-populated Odontoceti suborder to which our dolphins belong. This suborder consists of the dolphin, freshwater dolphin, sperm whale or cachalot, lesser sperm whale, bottle-nosed whale, narwhal or sea unicorn, white whale, pilot whale or blackfish, killer whale or grampus.

How I may proceed to pick from the half-hundred dolphins three or four types without offending someone who is in the process of proving Risso's dolphin is better or faster or nicer than Hector's dolphin, I don't know, so I will choose what most regard as the most common dolphins and look at where they live to give some reasonable idea of their immense spread.

For when we come to consider what could be happening in the seas of the world among a group of creatures with proven (in fact multiple) powers of communication, the fact that they are everywhere becomes, to put it very mildly, interesting.

Our now familiar friend *Tursiops truncatus*, the bottle-nosed dolphin, regards about half the existing sea space of the world as his home. Preferring relatively shallow waters, *Tursiops* may be found along the Atlantic coast of North America from Canada down to the Bay of Biscay and into the Mediterranean as far as the Adriatic. He uses the East African coast and the Indian Ocean. He can be found off Florida and in the St. Johns River; north across the Pacific in a broad band as far as Japan; off southern Greenland and Norway and south as far as South Australia, New Zealand and South Africa. The species is divided into a cold stenothermal northern race favoring the North Atlantic and a warm stenothermal southern group in the Pacific and Indian Oceans. Believed to be a product of the Upper Pliocene age in Europe, the northern *Tursiops* may have swum south through the "Suez Canal." No, that is not as impossible as it sounds. Apparently there was a natural Suez Canal in the Upper Pliocene. The division of the two groups occurred when this ancient sea gate resealed itself.

Tursiops alone would be enough to give the world a meaningful dolphin population, but he has brother and sister species which not only fill in the gaps he leaves but expand into other sea areas as well.

Delphinus delphis, the common dolphin, is aptly named. He may be found in any temperate sea throughout the world, and he swims in schools that make the word "vast" seem inadequate. Jacques Yves Cousteau, the twentieth century's Old Man of the Sea, has come very close to seeing it all, but still cannot repress his sense of wonder at the size of these dolphin swarms:

"When we sighted the school from afar, the water was churning as though it were boiling," Cousteau recounts, adding that his captain then reported an uncharted reef dead ahead. "It was not until we were closer that we realized that the 'reef' was an incredible assembly of dolphins—no fewer than 10,000 of them and perhaps as many as 20,000—leaping playfully into the air."

Another French marine expert, René G. Busnel, reported seeing schools of dolphins that filled the horizon for 30 or 40 miles!

That big black-and-white neo-villain *Orcinus orca,* the killer whale, may be found exhibiting what Ashley Montagu describes as "singular cunning and intelligence" from the Arctic to the Atlantic. He has a taste for cold seas and coastal waters but has been seen off the coast of Morocco and has even been known to steam up large rivers.

The famous Dutch cetologist Willem Dudock van Heel has perfected humane collection and transportation techniques for these huge dolphins, and on a recent expedition to Iceland described a herd that "stretched from horizon to horizon." *Orcinus orca* can grow as large as 35 feet and is one of the most attractively marked dolphins in the sea. It is a shiny jet black with a very large dorsal fin. The lower jaw is brilliant white, and there are two flags of white behind the eyes and another two at the base of the body trunk. Behind the dorsal fin, orcas have a grayish patch that looks like, and has been labeled, a saddle. Orcas are the only members of the cetacean species who undermine the dolphin's reputation for nonaggression. They will attack members of their own species and other animals and appear to be completely fearless. While most dolphins are naturally nervous out of water, orcas will surf in onto a beach to attack a seal, apparently having made the calculation that the next wave will save them from being stranded.

Herman Melville supports the orca's aggressive reputation in his chapter on cetology in *Moby-Dick*: "He is very savage. He sometimes takes the great Folio Whales by the lip, and hangs there like a leech, till the mighty brute is worried to death." Melville, however, then adds an interesting footnote: "Exception might be taken to the name bestowed upon this whale, on the grounds of its indistinctness. For we are all killers, on land and on sea: Bonapartes and sharks included."

Melville's intuitive rejection of orcas as unthinking killers is supported by contemporary evidence. They behave as amicably and placidly as other dolphins in captivity.

The Iceland catching team led by Dr. van Heel found that the orcas showed no aggression toward humans even when his divers entered the open end of a floating purse-seine net to move a young orca that minutes previously had been part of a wild herd into a lifting pontoon. That same animal has since been successfully flown to Holland where it now amicably, and seemingly contentedly, shares a habitat with its alleged natural enemies, other smaller dolphins and even seals.

It must be assumed that the orca's "killer" reputation is an exaggerated description of its normal eating pattern. Small dolphins do not need to hunt animals larger than fish for their food, but 35-foot dolphins occasionally do. Killer whales, when fed well in sea zoos, revert to the nonaggression pattern that is common to all dolphins.

As contemporary interest in dolphins blossomed, scientists discovered groups that were the obvious descendants of animals which survived the great cull of mammals in the last great ice age. Called the genus *Sotalia*, there are eleven separate types, but they all hug the coasts of warm continents or shelter in tropical rivers. Some of these animals have very long snouts like the throwbacks of the Amazon rivers, but in every other sense, including their size—*Sotalia plumbea*, inhabiting the Malabar Coast of India, is 8 feet long—are true sea dolphins. They may well represent the step from river to sea.

Other dolphins were found to have a particular liking for certain coastal features—hence the harbor porpoise, found cruising from eastern Canada to the Delaware and in the Baltic, the North Sea and the Mediterranean. My own interest in dolphins began with what I thought had to be a harbor porpoise during a three-month sojourn on Teceira Island in the Azores. We were there on an extraordinarily romantic marine archaeological expedition—to find Drake's famous flagship, the *Revenge*, which sank after an epic (and extremely foolhardy) attack on half the Portuguese fighting fleet.

We did not find the remains of the *Revenge*, but we did meet an awful lot of dolphins, since identified as common dolphins, who so enjoyed the ride on the bow waves of our diving boat that eventually they would enter Angra Harbour at 8:30 every morning to see whether we were going out that day. In fact they became a positive nuisance, because a secondary purpose of the expedition was to test a new type of shark gun. Hammerhead sharks are fairly common off the Azores, but our escort of dolphins never allowed us to get in the water with them. The dolphins had obviously decided that we did not know hammerheads bit people and as soon as we took our boat anywhere near a shark, the dolphins would chase them away.

Harbor porpoises have a distinctly human trait—they like the sun and follow it "on vacation." So as it wanes in the northern hemisphere they wander south and then back again as the seasons change.

And while we are on the subject of "porpoises," it is worth noting the difference. As has been said, they are dolphins and it would probably be less confusing if the word "porpoise" was dropped altogether. But for the record, a porpoise/dolphin is a small, beakless member of the Delphinidae with a triangular dorsal fin and spade-shaped teeth. It is black above and white below. The word is derived from the French *porcpoisson* ("pigfish"), which seems to me to be another good reason for dropping it.

As man's knowledge of the dolphin species increased, strange cousins were identified and added to the family Cetacea. Strangest, unquestionably, was the *Monodon monoceros*—the narwhal or sea unicorn. Swimming lazily in Arctic seas South of the icefields, the male has an immense tusk, as long as 9 feet.

This fearsome weapon seems almost to represent an optional extra. It has no parallels in the dolphin family and is not even centrally positioned. It sticks out from the left side of a bluntly rounded muzzle and is spirally grooved. The great irony of the sea unicorn/dolphin's tusk (which is the source of the unicorn of heraldry) is that it was obviously developed as a survival weapon but has very nearly resulted in the animal's extinction. It may have been some use against marine predators, but when man arrived on the scene it was a great curiosity and the narwhal was hunted mercilessly.

We found the blunt-nosed, submarine-shaped super-dolphin *Globiocephala melas*, otherwise known as the pilot, a gleaming black navigational expert. The pilot was accorded his title by square-rigged ship sailors who noted that they consistently swam safe passages through tricky, rock-strewn waters. Modern researchers were able to establish that the legend was well founded. When schools of these dolphins move off on a passage, massive groups stay together in the rear while one of their number—the pilot—moves ahead to find the best passage.

But again we must stop unless we are to disappear beneath the avalanche of our own information. There are white dolphins and brown ones and blue ones and greenish ones, dolphins with spots and dolphins with patches, dolphins with long beaks, small beaks and no beaks, dolphins with perfect eyes and dolphins that can't see. There are the dolphin throwbacks already discussed. There is even a dolphin in the Kamerun River that is a total vegetarian. Suffice it to say that where there is water there are dolphins. And there is a lot of water on this planet of ours—139 million square miles of it, in fact!

Although by the start of the '50s our knowledge of dolphins had increased tenfold, it had also begun to be suspected that we had done little more than identify the shape of this particular Pandora's box. What was in it, or for that matter, how to get the lid off, could only be guessed at.

For example, it is fairly common knowledge today that dolphins have a sonar or asdic system for locating objects by bouncing sound signals off them, and later in this book we will see that the sophistication of this system is still almost beyond man's ability to test it. But these signals were first recorded from dolphins as recently as 1953 by an American scientist, Woods, and it was several years later before Schevill and Laurence actually identified them as echo-locating sounds.

We also knew next to nothing about looking after dolphins properly, even though we were quite content to have them contained in pools, and many dolphins died. These deaths were as much the result of ignorance as of neglect. The dolphin, it turned out, suffers most of the health problems of man. His respiratory system is extremely delicate and he seems to catch various lung ailments very easily. He needs blood tests and shots and careful feeding, hygienically prepared food and a clean "house" to live in. His delicate skin produces bruises and lesions more quickly than man's, and he develops serious internal conditions that can only be treated by surgery.

And so caring men operated on dolphins, using proper anesthetics to ensure they suffered no pain. The dolphins died on the operating table. There can surely be no greater pointer to our ignorance of the species, even among these medical samaritans, than the fact that they killed dolphins by humane anesthetization—because they did not know that a dolphin must think before taking a breath, whereas man does it automatically. The anesthetics used in those early operations switched off the dolphin's mechanism and he died for want of air.

A new breed of dolphin doctors or marine veterinarians had to evolve alongside the new breed of marine circus animals. It was among these men that appreciation of gymnastic ability gave way to admiration, to confusion and finally to nagging doubts that man had finally come across something that was his equal and maybe something more.

In Europe, a veterinarian, David Taylor, found himself being called to the new dolphinariums, not because he was in any sense a dolphin doctor but because his speciality was exotic animals and the dolphinarium owners had at least come to the conclusion that dolphins were definitely exotic.

Man does not always learn by his mistakes but from this one

we did, and men like David Taylor found themselves jetting from one country to another, desperately finding out as much as they could, as quickly as they could, about dolphins. In a remarkably short time they established a medical routine for the animals.

It was not an easy assignment. The most basic parameters were confusing, like for example the "attitude" of the animals to painful treatment.

"They bear no grudges," Taylor points out. "I deal with chimpanzees and tigers and animals of advanced intelligence and the second time I go they remember me. Obviously I don't try to hurt them but I have to prick them with needles and things like that—and they remember! It's hard to get anywhere near them the second time. But dolphins, never!

"Even when I have to open an abscess, the next time, or even the same day, they immediately come to me. I've even considered that this might be plain stupidity, in spite of their obvious intelligence, but it isn't. It is too consistent. I think they realize there is no malevolence on our part. I'm not going to speculate exactly how but they realize that what we're doing has a purpose and whatever we do we're not trying to be sadistic in any sense and thus they accept it. Now a chimpanzee, who a lot of people place next to man in intelligence, he thinks I'm a terrible menace when next I appear with my hypodermic syringe."

Taylor's experience was being echoed by veterinarians all over the world (Plutarch's unselfish love of man?) and caused these men with scientific training to watch and wonder at many of the dolphin's more obvious attributes—and at a few that were not so obvious.

"I've often had the impression that one's moods, optimism or sometimes depression are communicable to dolphins; that somehow they can feel whether you, as it were, were willing things to go in a certain direction, and this is very important to us when dealing with medical matters. This applies to a limited degree with some other animals as well but with the dolphin particularly. You have these 'good' days when you somehow make a sort of contact. I don't know—we just seem to jel."

Taylor, with dolphin lives at stake, is a scientist who is obliged to move carefully, practicing known and tried methods. I was therefore somewhat surprised when he suddenly branched off into the "minefield"—telepathy!

"There is a possibility—just a possibility—that dolphins use some mechanism, call it telepathy if you like, to communicate between one another when they're in a group."

Frankly, why should an admission of this nature be so startling? As I have already noted, we did not know fifteen years ago that a "ping" from a dolphin was bringing it back a complex three-dimensional sonovision picture of almost everything around it. At best we suspected it. The fact of the matter is that scientific training conditions most scientists not to speculate and even condemns suspicion. This seems to me a complete contradiction of their role—they, of all people, must have inquiring minds, and to demand proof *before* speculation is ludicrous. I am more than a little certain that this book will be relegated by a number of fixed scientific minds to the school of the speculative, even the romantic. That would be very negative. If I am doing no more than asking the clinical scientist to reexamine his conceptual thinking, as the scientific establishment will endlessly question the findings of its own members, I am asking a serious "scientific" question. Especially if the weight of doubt and speculation has now reached such proportions as to constitute a body of evidence in its own right.

But in one particular human arena, scientific but at the same time pragmatic, the suspicions, speculations and doubts of the new generation of dolphin experts like David Taylor *were* noted. These people had vested interests—objects in the sea that were the only rivals in size to the huge whales: nuclear submarines.

When the military establishments of the Western world, in particular the navies of the front runners, America and Russia, heard the reports of the goings-on at dolphinariums, they stopped and listened and eventually acted.

Fifteen years after the move of the military in the direction of dolphins, they can afford to describe these activities in breezy

PR handouts. But when they happened, the moves described below in the current U.S. Navy handout were classified, and today's openhandedness cannot disguise the fact that military interest and investment expanded with ominous speed from a single tank to a multi-facilitied complex. Nor does it disguise the particular areas of interest.

The Navy's Marine Mammal Program had its origin in the acquisition in 1960, of a Pacific white-sided dolphin for hydrodynamic studies. Scientists of the Naval Ordance Test Station at China Lake in Pasadena, California, had heard accounts of the hydrodynamic efficiency of porpoises. Since NOTS was in the business (among other things) of designing and developing torpedoes, it seemed reasonable . . .

Facilities weren't good enough at NOTS, so the expansion program began.

NOTS scientists . . . looked out for an appropriate site at which to establish a small research facility. They found a site at Point Mugu where the Pacific Missile Range and Naval Missile Center were located. . . .

The show was on the road.

Primary interest was in Marine Mammals—the study of their specially developed senses and systems (such as sonar and deep diving physiology) and also how porpoises and sea lions might be used to perform useful tasks. . . .

We will review just what the Navy meant by "useful tasks" later in this book. In the meantime, its all go and expansion down at Point Mugu.

In 1967, the Point Mugu facility was transferred to a newly formed organization which was to become the Naval Underseas Research and Development Center with Headquarters in San Diego.

So seven years after acquiring its first dolphin, U.S. military interest had grown to a complete establishment—and what an establishment!

The major facilities of NUC were and are located at San Diego and Pasadena, with test facilities or laboratories at Long Beach, San Clemente Island, Morris Dam, Idaho, Cape Prince of Wales in Alaska, and Point Mugu. A laboratory was also established in Hawaii at the Marine Corps Air Station on Kaneohe Bay. . . .

Out of this multimillion-dollar complex, the Navy announced three significant headings in which it was most interested:

Organisms that can adversely effect Naval operations.

Organisms whose specially developed systems—sensory, physiological, or anatomical—might be considered as models for man-made analogs with improved characteristics over existing "hardware systems" (this is often termed bionics).

Organisms that might be used to perform underwater tasks more efficiently and effectively than human divers or man-made devices.

The dolphin had joined the U.S. Navy (and I regret to say, as his nature dictates, as a willing recruit) with a vengeance!

On the other side of the iron curtain, military interest got off to a slower start, but once it started there was again no stopping it.

Russia does not issue press handouts on its military activities, even when those activities have slipped far enough into the past to have no value to the enemy. But I am reliably informed that there are at least six institutions in the USSR actively studying cetaceans; the whole program is supervised and directed by the powerful Academy of Sciences of the USSR.

I have some information on what these institutions are up to which will fit into our account later, and recently I was lucky enough to find a Russian survey of data on dolphins, in which the authors unwittingly revealed the theme underlying Russia's interest. We must be thankful that inhibitions in one part of the world are not necessarily operative in another and that writers of official reports invariably reflect what is acceptable in their own countries.

Personally I feel there is no misinterpreting introductions from the Russian survey phrased as follows. Take special note of the last lines of the following two paragraphs.

Another set of problems [study of the dolphin's communications signals] . . . is being investigated with the aim of improving means of communication, of finding ways of setting up informational contact with animals and of controlling their behavior.

This next comment followed a review of brain data:

Alongside this aspect which belongs to the realm of theory, a practical need has now arisen, in connection with man's aim to probe the depths of the Ocean World, to discover the patterns governing the higher nervous activity of the dolphin. Because the animal is comparatively easy to tame and train, there is hope that it may be made to play the same role in the sea that the dog plays on land.

Without wishing to promote racial antagonism in a book designed to mitigate it, in the light of some of the experimental purposes to which Russian scientists have submitted dogs, I cannot allow a note of this nature to pass without comment.

It all added up to a huge, military-oriented, exploitive assault on the dolphin. Pandora's box was about to be levered open, if necessary, with some very blunt tools.

And the question which most intrigued them all was a nonsense—a contradiction of everything we knew that had been named after the British scientist who first suggested it: Gray's Paradox. In 1936 this Cambridge zoologist pointed out that somehow or other the dolphin was swimming seven times faster than his muscles would permit!

THREE

The Shape of Things to Come

THAT dolphins could swim very fast indeed, and that their movement through water was somehow different from that of any other solid object, had been variously noted long before Gray projected it as a mathematical impossibility.

Down the ages, fishermen had noted that the wake of their boats, moving on moonlit nights through "phosphorescence," was strangely different from the wakes left by the dolphins who sometimes came along for the ride. Whereas the speeding dolphins left two straight, glowing lines as their wake, the boat created a bumpy, broken pattern.

Jacques Yves Cousteau, in a book written with Phillipe Doile, acknowledges that it was the sight of dolphins "at speed" that first lured him to the animals. He was on the bridge of a new cruiser, the *Primauguet*, moving at a speed of 33.5 knots:

I was standing on the bridge, enthralled by the performance of the mighty cruiser as it cut through the sea with incredible violence. Then I glanced to starboard. A school of dolphins was alongside. I watched and suddenly I realized that the dolphins were moving faster than the *Primauguet* . . . they were passing her! . . . swimming at a speed of no less than 50 miles per hour!

That was forty years ago. Since then I have had many encounters with dolphins, but I have never forgotten my first impression of those great mammals as they materialized in front of *Primauguet*'s stem—faster, and infinitely more maneuverable, than the best machines that human ingenuity had yet been able to devise."

Instantly Cousteau moves to the prime motivation—have they got something we haven't? This single consideration was the factor underlying man's new interest in dolphins when we rediscovered the species as a result of the dolphinarium boom.

The universities of Oxford and Cambridge have always been famous for their "pure" research—scientific exploration in search of essential understanding—and no one has ever suggested that Dr. J. Gray, who was to ask the big "how" about dolphin speeds, was motivated by anything other than zoological curiosity. His research was, however, conducted in 1936, only three years before Germany went to war with the rest of Europe, and it is an extreme coincidence, if nothing more, that the factor most bothering the powerful British Navy was Germany's advanced submarine fleet of U-boats.

Be that as it may, this Cambridge scientist threw all the dolphin experts of his time into high confusion when he produced his paradox. He was able to show that if the dolphin was encountering the same drag as other solid objects moving through water, it would need somehow to produce *seven times* the power it apparently possessed to produce the speeds of which it was known to be capable. Or more simply, the dolphin was swimming seven times faster than the mathematics said were possible!

To get some idea of the revolutionary nature of that statement, pause for a moment and consider the somewhat ridiculous sight of a man standing flapping his arms. Nothing happens. Add a couple of suitable airfoils and increase the power of his flapping arms by seven times and something magnificent would probably happen. You would be watching the first flying man!

The key to Gray's Paradox was the drag factor, called turbulence. The existence of turbulence in water has been of interest to man since we first went down to the sea in ships, although it is still a hard phenomenon to visualize. It might help to imagine a "race" of steel ball bearings running smoothly in a track around an object. If the race runs smoothly, the movement is continuous, unbroken and swift—a laminar flow. If anything goes wrong with the stream of bearings, if they start to pile up and clog, total confusion hits the system. It ceases to be a smooth effective flow and becomes a jumble. Solid objects striking through water, and the grip of these objects on the water, break up the smooth flow of the liquid and creates bumpy turbulence like our disrupted race of bearings. It's possible to calculate the "turbulence-creating" effect of objects in water and give the object a number, called a Reynolds number.

Gray calculated the Reynolds number, or turbulence-creating factor, of a 6-foot common dolphin, using a rigid 6-foot model for comparison. He also had to make a reasonable calculation of the power of the dolphin's muscle structure, and he chose the most powerful human model he could think of—a trained oarsman.

Putting these equations together—a muscle-power output equivalent to a straining oarsman in a racing boat against the drag of water on his dolphin model—produced the paradox. There was no way the dolphin's muscles could overcome the drag of water sufficiently to produce a speed of 15 knots—the best-authenticated top speed for a common dolphin. It was not only impossible, but ridiculous, because when Gray took his equations one step further he was able to calculate that the dolphin would need to create *seven times* the power it possessed to overcome the drag it would be encountering at 15 knots!

At first Gray's Paradox was treated with the open skepticism that would seem to be science's conditioned reflex to an idea that expands but does not detail new areas of possibility. It was suggested that the test conditions were inadequate. Gray himself had added a note to his findings which hinted that something odd was happening to the water in the vicinity of the rear end of the dolphin—"and to this extent it seems conceivable that the flow past the surface of the actively moving dolphin is much less turbulent than is the case when the inert organism is towed through the water"—but this note aided rather than silenced critics of the paradox. They suggested his Reynolds numbers were wrong and that the rear end of the animal should be left out of the equation.

A number of scientists questioned his "power pack"—the trained oarsman. Taggart claimed that the oarsman needed some of his muscle power to sit upright and suggested Gray consider a racing cyclist. Gray took this suggestion seriously and embarked on an exhaustive, and exhausting, series of experiments—all of which showed that the power available to the dolphin from its known muscle structure was no greater than that of trained athletes, be they pole vaulters or broad jumpers.

Someone suggested that the common dolphin was a somewhat lazy swimmer, so Gray investigated other species and discovered that *Stenella attenuata* was able to develop two and a half times the power output of a trained human athlete, which was interesting, but did nothing to qualify the original paradox. It got to the point eventually where alternative theories were being advanced almost as if science was determined *not* to accept that the dolphin had something special.

But paradoxes are like burrs under the saddle of science, and others worried away at the problem. And by this time, investigators sponsored and financed by the military establishments had entered the field. They had a motivation which lifted them beyond scientific competition. Accepting the possibility that Gray's Paradox was valid, or at worst, half valid, they had started to make their own calculations and theoretical applications of whatever it was dolphins were doing to produce speed without drag. They created hypothetical models of the effect such a facility would have if it could be applied to submarines, with results that caused the funds for research to pour in like a flood.

Submarines then, and for that matter now, were the equivalent of Gray's rigid model of comparison. In spite of the most efficient streamlining human engineers could create (and special paint surfaces, coatings and facings), submarines performed more or less exactly as their Reynolds number said they would. A given size of engine in a given solid object would create a known amount of turbulence and move at a certain speed.

The attraction for the military scientists of the present era was obvious. Get a submarine to perform like a dolphin and you open a huge, revolutionary field of possibilities. Your submarines could either go seven times faster—70 knots instead of 10—or half that speed with huge savings of engine size, space and fuel consumption. Or you could build huge submarines capable of carrying even larger loads of nuclear hardware with no great increase in power!

Small wonder that Gray's Paradox so excited the military scientists. The nuclear submarine was the prime weapon for both the superpowers. If one of them could unlock the paradox and apply it to their fleets the entire balance of power would alter overnight, giving the finder a lead so massive as to almost amount to instant victory in the psychological battle that has been going on since actual war ceased in the West in 1945.

And the more the paradox was examined—and by the middle '60s, science had decided to accept the possibility—the more it appeared Gray had got it right. All the tests showed that dolphin speeds were very high; that Cousteau, Gray and all the others who had judged the speed of the animals had not been imagining things. The suggestions that these speeds were a freak phenomenon—racing starts sustained for brief spurts by some special metabolic factor in dolphins—were disproved by the experiments of C. L. Johannssen and J. A. Harder, who showed that *Stenella* dolphins could maintain a speed of 18 knots for periods varying between 8 and 25 minutes (sufficient to keep the paradox valid), and that the pilot whale could steam along for extended periods at 22 knots while the killer whale was cruising comfortably at 20 knots. In 1966, Dr. Kenneth Norris appeared to have punched something of a hole in Gray's Paradox in favor of the metabolism school; he and others showed that *Tursiops gilli* swam faster in short bursts than for extended periods. But when the actual speeds were revealed, 21.9 kilometers per hour at the slow end and an incredible 29.9 kilometers per hour under acceleration, we were firmly back in the realm of paradox. All that these tests showed was that some dolphins swam faster for short periods, not how they did it. The elimination of stultifying drag was still a puzzle.

So dolphins were copied, examined, made to run bizarre races—and literally taken apart.

A huge school of researchers set themselves the task of cracking Gray's Paradox, and there are at least five hundred learned scientific papers now on file as evidence of the challenge which the dolphin had finally presented to man—a challenge that, in a sense, was the first competitive exercise between the two species, dolphin and man. Whereas the ancient Greeks had been content to watch and wonder, contemporary man seemed intellectually irritated that an animal had presented evidence of superiority.

Species status was at stake and, inevitably, dead dolphins, many the result of malpractice in dolphinariums, some the victims of ignorance such as the mistakes with anesthesia, arrived on the dissecting tables of the new marine laboratories. Surgical knives laid bare tissues and bone that reminded us again of our common evolutionary heritage.

Tiny bones found at the extreme end of the dolphin's body were recognized as atrophied remains of the hip girdle and leg bones of a mammal that had once moved on land. In whale corpses, odd bumps were noted which later turned out to be "leg bones" even closer to man's. In a whale killed near Vancouver these ancient relics of a four-limbed animal were nearly a meter long.

Some of the corpses were coffins of the unborn, and these fetuses brought our common heritage poignantly closer. The embryo of the whale was seen to have a tail with no flukes and four limb studs on buds—startlingly like a human embryo at an age of a few weeks. More developed fetuses extended the similarity—"older" whale embryos had distinctly humanoid characteristics like nipples and a penis hanging outside the body (streamlined flaps later enclose the penis in the adult male whale), hair on the head and very distinct "finger bones" in the half-formed flippers.

Dissection also revealed the magnificent machine that is the modern dolphin's body. Immense muscles and straplike sinews encase the skeleton; tissues stronger than steel and more resilient than nylon. The whole rear end of the animal moves up and down with tremendous energy, and this movement is not confined, as with most fishes, simply to the tail. In fact the tail itself proves to be a sophisticated mechanism combining all man knew of marine propulsion systems with a dolpin "extra."

As Herman Melville had noted in his description of a dolphin as "a spouting fish with a horizontal tail," the animal has a propulsion mechanism which lies flat in the water, whereas the tails of most fish lie, and work, sideways.

And the dolphin's tail is not a simple triangle flapping up and down in the water. There are two cleverly shaped dished flukes that move in a complex sculling motion producing a sophisticated, powerful equivalent of the single-oar rowing action used by the gondoliers of Venice. The action is so powerful, in fact, that scientists have calculated it is more efficient than the screw used on ships, and attempts have been made to copy it on experimental vessels. Moreover, the dolphins have built a feathering mechanism into their tails. This is also a trick used by human oarsmen, who turn their wrists as the blades of their oars leave the water so that the flat surface is presented parallel to the water and the oarsman is not slowed or pitched out of the boat should his oar hit the water—a mistake known as "catching a crab." Dolphins don't catch crabs because their tails don't leave the water, but their tails, in particular the tips of the flukes, bend upward to ease the downward movement of the tail, then lock flat as the dolphin pushes upward, presenting a solid, flat, and very powerful driving surface to the water.

But none of this provided a single answer to Gray's Paradox. He was an expert anatomist himself, and he knew all about the dolphin's machine-body.

The fact remained that even with this advanced muscle structure, the dolphin should not be able to swim faster than 10 to 12 knots, because of the resistance his solid body should create in water. Of course, that assumed that man knew all there was to know about the resistance of water on solid bodies.

But did we? The more we studied the problem, the more the contradictions emerged. The most dramatic piece of evidence was discovered in the log of a whaling captain. He recorded that a female blue whale, after being pursued at full speed, had been successfully harpooned. The engines of the 90-foot, twin-screwed chaser were immediately put full astern. Despite the fact that the whale (and this is a toothed whale, or "big-dolphin" type) had a ¼-ton harpoon trailing half a mile of 4-inch rope embedded in its back, she proceeded to pull the ship at a speed of 5 knots for eight and a half hours!

Finally, human scientists were forced to face up to the problem. Gray's Paradox was valid. Somehow or other dolphins were overcoming what they had considered a fixed physical principle—that when a solid object moves through water, the water clings to it, forming small, restrictive eddies, called turbulence. Streamlining limits turbulence but cannot eliminate this drag, and in any event, dolphin streamlining, although excellent, could not eliminate it sufficiently to resolve Gray's Paradox.

At first it was decided that the secret lay in the dolphin's skin. This, as it happened, was an enlightened guess, but this first avenue of research turned out to be a blind alley.

For two years, beginning in 1960, Dr. M. O. Kramer built, to the best of his ability, copies of the outer layers of the skin of dolphins, a resilient-elastic skin cover with a liquid filler. These artificial dolphin skins were in fact a double layer of rubber, trapping a network of fluid-filled canals, and at first it was thought that Kramer had cracked Gray's Paradox. His giant contraceptives resulted in a 40 percent reduction in drag. The Russian scientist Sokolov pointed out, accurately, that Kramer's skin covers were a very poor copy of the dolphin's skin, but this still did not answer the fact that 60 percent of the paradox remained unsolved.

It was almost back to square one, with the scientists lapsing into answers as paradoxical as Gray's first proposition. Had you asked a scientist in the early '60s whether they had arrived at a decision on the subject of the dolphin's speed through water, the answer (as once happened to me) was, "Well, yes and no."

In 1963, Dr. Peter Purves left the monstrous graveyard that is the Whale Room at the British Museum of Natural History and traveled to Harderwijk, Holland, where Dr. Willem van Heel was financing some of the most advanced cetacean research in Europe from the profits of a unique dolphinarium.

This huge, flying-saucer-shaped structure, supported by canals and secondary pools, is perhaps the most successful attempt in the world to combine the two realities of contemporary dolphin interest—entertainment for which the public is prepared to pay, and dolphin research, for which it is most reluctant to pay.

Purves and van Heel had decided it was high time an all-out assault on Gray's Paradox should be mounted, using modern techniques and equipment. They began by painstakingly building a "perfect" wooden dolphin, suspecting rightly that Gray's Paradox did not have a single solution but was probably an amalgam of characteristics: shape, metabolism, skin—and the abstract.

It was an ideal combination of talents. Purves knew as much as anyone in the world of cetacean anatomy, and van Heel was a good zoologist with a school of well-cared-for dolphins at his disposal. They brought in a third party, A. Jonk, of the Ship Model Test Station, the Netherlands, an expert in model building and solid test structures, to complete the team.

While the accurate measuring of a dolphin and the conversion of these fine measurements to a wooden copy went on, Purves and van Heel reviewed all the experimental and theoretical data then existing on the subject of dolphin hydrodynamics, concluding:

> There were a number of important omissions without which it would be impossible to approach an accurate assessment of the problem. For instance, in Gray's paper there are no technical details of towing experiments with an actual model of a dolphin so that the distinction between skin "friction" and residuary resistance cannot be made.

They also noted (a classic understatement) that all the available data showed a somewhat rudimentary knowledge of cetacean anatomy and physiology.

A closer examination of the dolphin from which Lang had taken his speeds, in particular of the tank in which the dolphin had been swimming, showed conclusively that these conditions were far from ideal. The tank had a maximum depth of 6.5 feet, and from his knowledge of the dolphin's anatomy, Purves realized that this particular dolphin could only have been moving under about half his muscle power. Had he brought his main epaxial locomotor muscles into play he would almost certainly have hit the bottom of the tank. Not that this conclusion helped the Hardewijk team resolve the paradox—extra speed made it worse—but at least it showed that Gray's finding bore investigation.

They decided to try to take the paradox apart piece by piece, beginning with the way water moved over the surface of the dolphin. They knew that the skin factor was important from Kramer's partial successes with rubber simulacra but suspected that the pieces of the jigsaw were numerous and it was time to start again from basic principles.

Their model was shaped from a full-grown *Tursiops truncatus* (bottle-nosed) dolphin, a member of the Harderwijk team which had been caught in the Gulf of Mexico off the Florida Keys. As this first stage of research was aimed at water movement across the body, the fin and flippers were left off the model. The tail was copied and attached with a hinge, the specific gravity of the "tail" adjusted to that of the water.

Measuring devices were set into the model, then covered with brass plates exactly in line with the rest of the surface, and the whole wooden structure carefully varnished with a waterproof lacquer. The final model was a copy of the original, accurate to three decimal points.

In fact, van Heel and Purves were also testing a theory of their own in the general context of their attack on Gray's Paradox. In experiments conducted in 1963 and 1968 they had decided that the power stroke in the dolphin's tail movement was the upstroke, rather than the downstroke which had been assumed to be the motor movement. Purves had spotted the inverse logic of the tail from his knowledge of muscles and how they worked, and the two had found some confirmation of the theory when they examined the dolphin's tail and found that the flukes feathered (bent away from the water) as the tail moved down. If the theory of the upstroke was right it would radically alter concepts of how water moved across the dolphin's body. It would not flow horizontally along the animal but would be pushed obliquely upward.

One further item of anatomical knowledge existed in the minds of the research team ahead of their tests. Earlier dissection of dolphins had revealed that the epidermis (the outer layer of skin cells) of cetaceans is keyed to the dermis (the true skin) in a series of ridges similar to the palms of the hands and feet of the primates and man. In dolphins, however, these skin ridges are so fine as to not be visible to the human eye, and it had always been assumed that they played no part in the reduction of turbulence. Kramer had actually stated this as a definite fact.

But in 1963, Purves, the anatomist, had taken a very careful look at these dermal ridges. Previous examinations of isolated scraps of dolphin skin had led to the belief that they ran parallel with the long axis of the dolphin's body, but Purves' study showed otherwise. The dermal ridges ran in various directions, and he suspected that these lines were in fact the streamlines for the water passing over the dolphin's body.

Thus when their finished wooden dolphin was carefully lowered into the experimental tank at Harderwijk, Purves and van Heel were actually hopeful of proving a theory rather than a simple examination of the unknown aspects of Gray's Paradox. They thought, from their knowledge of the tail movement and their suspicions about dermal ridges being guidelines to water flow, that the dolphin was moving water up and across his body rather than along it in a way which would provoke the most turbulence.

With the help of a pot of paint, they were soon proved right. They dabbed a low-viscosity coating on various parts of the model, towed it at a speed of 6.14 millimeters per second and watched what happened to the paint.

Ironically, the whole complicated exercise (it took much effort to build the model and mount it on a carefully corrected towing structure) could have been avoided had Purves and van Heel known the true significance of certain marks that occur on the flanks of all dolphins. Take a very careful look at a dolphin and you will see these whitish marks rising up their sides toward the rear of the dorsal fin. This is where water goes when the dolphin moves through it.

The Harderwijk paint job proved this conclusively, as Purves explained:

In a rigid body like a submarine, the water passes straight from one end of the structure to the other. But in the dolphin it does no such thing. Along the back of the dolphin there is a thin ridge and the water sweeps backwards and upwards and separates over the ridge.

In a rigid body, if you like a submarine, once the water has passed the object's maximum cross section—its widest point—it forms into a very large eddy which we call "form drag." Because the dolphin is sweeping the water up on both sides of its body and breaking it off as a thin eddy there is effectively no form drag at all.

The upstroke of the tail was assisting this movement of water, as was the dolphin's whole swimming movement, which is a long fluctuation of the body from head to tail.

The down stroke of the tail is very gentle, in fact just a passive stroke. The flukes curl upwards and spill the water sideways and upwards. The effect of that is to keep the water flowing up the body all the time and this again prevents the formation of very large turbulent eddies.

It is with some relief that one may report that while Purves and van Heel made a considerable hole in Gray's Paradox it has not immediately resulted in the application of their discoveries to submarines. In some senses their experiments pushed that horrific possibility even further into the future, in that human engineering is many years away from being able to build an elastic metal structure that could echo the flexible swimming movement of the dolphin's body, although I have heard reports that a barge was built in a Communist-bloc country with the equivalent of a dolphin tail as its propulsion system, and that this system worked very well.

But apart from showing how water moves across the dolphin's body and that the dermal ridges are in line with these flows (both considerable steps forward), what exactly had they proved, and to what degree had they cracked Gray's Paradox?

They had done about half the job. They had explained how the dolphin overcomes form drag—the resistance a solid body creates when it moves through water. The measuring devices embedded in the body of their wooden dolphin had shown that when swimming at high speeds the dolphin's body came into its own as an extremely sophisticated hydrodynamic shape—certainly a better one than man had managed to invent. In fact the Harderwijk experiments showed that both the model and the live dolphin were hydrodynamically more efficient than an equivalent "body of revolution," which is the term used to describe man's best attempt at streamlining.

But as seems to be the case with all dolphin research, the Dutch "Trogan dolphin" also opened up another and somewhat dramatic area of doubt. The equations indicated that this superior hydrodynamic ability came into its own only at high speeds. The fact had to be faced that the basic shape of the bottle-nosed dolphin, and, it may be assumed, of other dolphin species, was not so good at speeds below 15 knots.

The team also reexamined some of the earlier research on the central "power pack" of dolphins. They put together known information about Lang's test animal (that it weighed 90.7 kilograms) and reliable speed trials by Johannsen and Harder which had shown this particular dolphin species to be capable of sustained swimming at 15 knots for twenty minutes. Purves applied his anatomy knowledge to the animal and concluded that a maximum of 20 percent could be called "propulsive muscle." They concluded the proper output per kilogram of muscle would be 5.8 kilograms meters/second. The reworking of this equation indicated immediately that the dolphin had a better power pack than man. So they examined Wilkie's human example—the trained cyclist—and studied the power output of such an athlete working flat out at a cranking machine. Assuming 20 kilograms of muscle being employed by the athlete—his output per kgm. of muscle was only 1.9 kilograms meters/second. Or more simply, the muscles of dolphins produce almost three times the power of the fittest man's muscles!

It may be, although this was never stated by the Harderwijk

team, that they suspected that the unsolved part of Gray's Paradox—the excess of speed over muscular potential that even their hydrodynamic revelations had not answered—could be attributed to the dolphin's extra-powerful metabolism. Indeed, Purves and van Heel hinted strongly in this direction in the official report of their research program:

> The muscle fibres of cetaceans are essentially similar in structure to those of terrestrial animals but their metabolism has been altered in a way not yet fully understood. Thus the oxygen consuming, restitution phase can be delayed for relatively long periods during which the muscles work anaerobically. It is not possible therefore to estimate the energy output in terms of simultaneous oxygen consumption as has been done with terrestrial mammals. In this respect the muscles may be *less* efficient than those of the trained athletes.

And that is about where they were forced to leave it, with half the puzzle solved but with the other half pushed even further into the unknown.

Ironically, another English anatomist who also used the Harderwijk facilities for some of his field studies during the period of the Purves/van Heel project was about to make an extraordinary suggestion as to how dolphins might be finding their extra speed.

Professor Harrison is probably the most eminent anatomy specialist in Britain, and it is no coincidence that he works out of the same university as did Dr. Gray—Cambridge. In 1974 he produced a complex, carefully hedged scientific paper worded in such a way as to make it almost incomprehensible to any but the expert anatomist. It dealt with the outer layers of the epithelium in cetaceans, advised the world that this layer was fully "keratinized" and went on to consider the quantity of "mucopolysaccharides" in these layers.

Reduced to lay language, what Harrison was in fact saying was that he had evidence to suggest that the dolphin might be swimming out of its own skin!

Anyone who has swum with dolphins knows that they have a skin of a superb, smooth texture, and the fact that the animal has such perfect control of its movements results in an impression of being stroked with a vibrant swathe of cool silk. Admittedly such an experience is rare but it can be visualized by anyone who has seen these silvered animals slide from the water in the lights of a dolphin show.

Others had turned their attention to the skin several years before Harrison was able to produce his hypothesis. Apart from Kramer's rubber skins, a group of American scientists did comprehensive research in the early '60s aimed at discovering how the flexibility and mobility of the skin's surface affected the stability of the currents in the boundary layer of water around the dolphin's skin. In the middle '50s, F. S. Essapian and P. Tomilin had noted that the dolphin's skin "undulated" as it moved through the water and that these movements might stabilize the laminar flow in the boundary area. Schlichting speculated that drag was being reduced by a change in temperature in the boundary layer, and some scientists came close to the Harrison area of research when they asked questions about the effect of the desquamatory cells of the outer layer of the epidermis.

But none of them conceived of anything as revolutionary as Harrison's skin-shedding dolphin. And I must put it on record that this clinical don would never have expressed it in those terms either. I was given the description by one of Professor Harrison's assistants, an English veterinarian, Andrew Greenwood, who explained that the Cambridge team had made detailed examinations using high-powered microscopes of the outer layers of the skin of dolphins, discovering that they were alive when they reached the surface, unlike man's, which are "hard and cornified."

These live dolphin cells were flat and very large—"a bit like cornflakes if you look at them from above." (That description relates to shape, not size!) Between these cells in the live state, the Cambridge electron microscopes showed a muscanous substance which was not only visible under enlargement but could also be detected biochemically on the surface of the dolphins.

"Two things seem to have happened," Greenwood explained.

"One is that this muscanous substance reaches the surface of the dolphin between the cells of the skin, and the cells themselves lose their connection between one another and become loose on the surface. You can in fact rub them off with your finger, and if you rub a dry dolphin hard enough you can get a brownish-gray scale. This is loose skin; live cells but spare skin coming away from the surface of the animal.

"It appears to work like this. When the dolphin accelerates from a standing start, the loose skin that has built up on the surface of the body is left behind, and the water is left working on that loose skin.

"But the dolphin is long gone!

"And the removal of all these cells from the surface leaves this slimy substance underneath which again helps the dolphin to slide forward through the water. This prevents the normal laminar flow of water over the surface from breaking up into the turbulent eddies which would hold him back."

I had been picturing this process in my mind as he described it and suddenly there before me in my mind's eye were two dolphins—one, the real animal at speed, the other a transparent ghost. As it turned out I should have been imagining a series of ghosts!

"The shedding is so microscopic you would not be able to see it—and it's probably a continuous process as the dolphin moves through the water."

There it was. The dolphin's speed was no longer a paradox. They possessed a body stripped by evolution and fifty million years of development in the sea to a hydrodynamic foil that was more efficient than anything man had ever designed; the whole clad in a removable friction jacket that even the most optimistic of today's engineers cannot believe may be copied with man's existing technology. For the time being the dolphin will remain the fastest thing in the sea, and our most advanced submarines limping cripples by comparison. A situation which fills me with a considerable feeling of relief.

But the cracking of Gray's Paradox had at least moved the dolphin into a new dimension in men's minds. Twenty years of committed research by perhaps a hundred scientists in this one area created not only a new sense of inquiry but a growing body of respect for the dolphin's extraordinary abilities; a respect that is well represented by Andrew Greenwood's reverent description of dolphins:

"We feel that the dolphin family as a group are supreme. They have complete control in their own environment. They are probably the most finely adapted animal in the natural universe." And he added a line which I hope will indicate to the ghosts of Aristotle and Pliny that they may stop turning in their graves. "A very classic and beautiful animal."

In this eulogy Greenwood identifies the core of modern man's reawakened interest. As recently as the '60s our experience of dolphins was on the surface, literally and figuratively. We knew that the dolphins who broke water alongside ships were our masters in terms of speed. But what else were they up to? What was happening under the surface of the waves? When Greenwood refers to "complete control of their own environment" he is condensing a series of discoveries about the dolphin in his own kingdom that were to make Gray's Paradox seem like grade-school homework.

FOUR

Lost Horizons

IN the same period as man is rediscovering and counting the dolphin he has also started a somewhat more dramatic count of himself.

The census of world populations in the '50s validated a theory advanced a century previously by Thomas Robert Malthus, and it was realized that if the Malthusian Armageddon of extinction from overpopulation was to be headed off, new food areas would have to be found.

But where? Two-thirds of the world's population was already hovering close to the starvation threshold, and there were no new continents to be conquered and farmed. All that was left was the vast area covered by sea. Eventually these undeveloped acres would have to be used somehow.

But the sea was a totally alien environment for man, and it was quickly discovered just how difficult a conquest of the sea would be. It is in fact easier to walk on the face of the moon than on the deep beds of the ocean, and our need required not just a short exploratory walk for science's sake but a complete underwater life-style that would support farms, mines and processing facilities.

Here the gap which exists between the two prime mammals, dolphin and man, even though we share an ancestry, begins to make itself dramatically evident. Whereas the cetaceans have spent the last fifty million years adapting themselves to life in the sea, man has spent his two million essentially afraid of it.

The changes go infinitely deeper than the shedding of limbs and the development of tails and flukes. Inside the dolphin, complex, finite changes of metabolism have also been going on—changes to do with the use of air, pressure and depth. Man was eons behind in this race, as our first tentative steps underwater proved.

The submariner is a phenomenon of this century, and the free-swimming "frogman" an even more recent form. The first aqualung was developed by Jacques Yves Cousteau as recently as 1943, and our entire knowledge of the terrors of the deep, the very real dangers of what the sea can do to the delicate fabric of man, is no more than twenty years old.

When my interest in the sea and its organisms grew beyond the point where I was content to watch the waves and fish around in rock pools, I took a scuba-training course—a vital prerequisite for any venturing underwater. The manual of instruction I was given to study long before I was ever allowed near deep water read like the script of a thriller movie.

In alphabetical order one encounters "air embolism"—damage to the lungs caused by air expanding when a diver, using an aqualung, holds his breath on ascending. "Anoxia"—lack of oxygen in the blood and body which may be caused by holding the breath too long. Underwater it can lead to drowning. "Bends"—illness caused by dissolved nitrogen forming bubbles in the blood or body tissue if too rapid an ascent is made. "Decompression"—the need to ascend slower to eliminate bubbles of gases that dissolve in the blood and body tissue. "Ear pressure"—pain that may be felt through unequal pressure on either side of the eardrum. "Hyperventilation"—the danger of taking too many deep breaths, which can cause death from anoxia. "Nitrogen narcosis"—a dangerous effect caused by the nitrogen in compressed air, which results in near hallucinations and inhibits the ability to cope with emergencies.

So it goes on—a panoply of proof that man in the sea is figuratively and literally out of his depth. And we are not really talking of any great depth—these are descriptions of the difficulties we encounter at depths of between 12 feet and less than 200. Only with years of complicated training, supported by every scrap of technology available, can man go deeper than 300 feet with any safety. This technology and its associated hardware—cumbersome diving vehicles and exotic breathing mixtures of gases based on a high content of helium—reduces man, the deep diver, to a tool that is about one step away from complete incompetence.

But the oceans of our planet are on average 12,566 feet deep! It is in every sense another world.

Small wonder then that the few divers prepared to brave these hazards and the scientists concerned with diving technology noted with interest that the sea mammals, the dolphins and in particular the great whales, appeared to have few of our problems even though, like man, they breathe air.

One scientist put the obvious possibility into words—wondering if the dolphin could "be made to help man as a sheepdog of the sea."

No one suffered any delusions as to how much the technology needed to support man's advance into the sea was going to cost, and inevitably these early research programs became the special purview of the military—in particular, the navy departments. This applied internationally, in Russia, in Europe and, in particular, in America, where, late into the space race, the U.S. government was, and still is, first in the field of "aquanautics." Americans even seemed to have recognized the like problems of the alien environments of deep space and the deep ocean, for America's first serious venture into the sea, aptly named the "Man-in-the-Sea Program," was led by a former astronaut, Scott Carpenter.

This program, initiated in 1965, was called Sealab Two. For the record, Sealab One, conducted a year earlier, was a tentatively financed exercise in underwater living which the official Navy record was later to label "primitive" and came to an abrupt end "as a result of an impending tropical storm."

Sealab Two was something else. And if I seem to be straying from my subject, Sealab Two was to become the first and still the most convincing example of man and dolphin working for mutual advantage.

As a start, the program was properly financed. Scientists and technologists, working to a seven-month deadline, began to build a "habitat" which would allow man to live and work underwater for extended periods at what, for man, was an extreme depth—205 feet.

The vehicle they eventually conceived looked like a huge section of drainpipe but it was in fact a complex "sea-space" capsule with its own very special life-support systems. Its resemblance to a vehicle designed to explore an alien planet is remarkable. It had "locks" to allow movement from one environment to another. It had support vehicles in much the same way as the lunar lander had a command ship in orbit around the moon. It had surface backup (in this case the Scripps Institute of La Jolla, California, 3,000 feet away on land) as the astronauts who bounced on the moon had Mission Control, Houston.

Only its purpose was more, shall we say, purpose-full. We were not on this occasion going to another planet to catch up in the space race. Sealab Two was a serious, determined, first step for man into an alien environment in which the American government knew it had the lead, as it revealed by the description Secretary to the Navy Paul H. Nitze chose for the project:

> I doubt if many realized the full significance of this pioneer effort to support human life and essential activity in the earth's most hostile environment.
>
> Sealab Two involved every phase of engineering including the development of new materials and techniques, the fabrication of sophisticated equipment and the solution to unique physiological and psychological problems.
>
> It should be a matter of pride to all of us that the Navy was able to provide the full spectrum of capabilities necessary to secure the success of such an enterprise.

And Jingoism aside, Nitze was right. It was a considerable achievement designed for a pragmatic purpose—the first assault on the next frontier, a vital frontier for the burgeoning race of man.

Sealab's success puts us at the threshold of an expanding capability for military operation on the continental shelf. Of equal importance to the welfare of nations, it increases our capabilities in the extraction of chemicals and minerals from the sea, the tending of pipelines, cables and underwater installations, the culture of marine life for food, and of course, the extension of geophysical exploration and the general advancement of earth sciences.

But having allowed Paul Nitze his superlatives (accurate, so far as they go) it must also be stated that Sealab Two would have been nothing but a paddle in a duck pond had it not been for the assistance of an obliging dolphin. To see this dolphin, a freak called Tuffy, in the right context, we must backtrack a year or so.

As the Navy's "General Summary of the Marine Mammal Program" shows, U.S. military interest in the working capability of the dolphin began in 1960 with the acquisition of a Pacific white-striped dolphin for hydrodynamic studies.

The animal was acquired by the Naval Ordnance Test Station (NOTS) at China Lake and Pasadena, California, a department concerned, among other things, with the design and development of torpedoes. With traditional military imagination it named this first animal Notty.

Notty turned out to be something of a disappointment. Swimming in the 315-foot torpedo towing tank in San Diego, Notty never achieved speeds higher than 15 knots, and Navy scientists began to question the rumors of dolphin speeds. They suspected, and rightly, that the confined conditions in the tank might be adversely affecting the dolphin's swimming capability, and in search of a better test site, they came to Point Mugu, the site of the Pacific Missile Range and Naval Missile Center.

Notty was not able to improve his speeds significantly, but two new Navy recruits, a pair of bottle-nosed dolphins, Peg and Keiki, more than justified the move to the new location, in particular the use of the open lagoon that adjoined Point Mugu, and gave the researchers their first opportunity to try out dolphins in a space more closely resembling their normal sea environment. Peg and Kieki not only swam faster than the Navy's first recruit but were successfully trained to follow boats and "work" for the first time in the equivalent of open-sea conditions.

But all this was rendered academic by the arrival at Point Mugu of Tuffy—or as he was first named, Tuf Guy—the first, and to my knowledge only, "star" to ever engrave his personality and extraordinary ability on the hardbitten scientific front of U.S. Navy research.

Tuffy joined the Navy program in May 1964 from a seaside amusement park in Santa Monica. No one knows what had happened to Tuffy at this park, but the fact remains that he appeared determined to contradict everything that had been said of dolphins since the time of Aristotle. As Point Mugu's senior veterinarian, Sam H. Ridgeway, was to remark, "Maybe we have the world's first man-eating porpoise on our hands."

In fact, what they had was the first truly aware dolphin—an animal possibly frustrated and confused by amusement-park trivia who, when he found himself presented with what must have seemed an extension of these mindless tricks, decided to resist, bite and butt—to the alarm of researchers used to dolphins exhibiting nothing but "forgiving friendship."

Only when a woman researcher, Deborah Duffield, made the enlightened decision to treat Tuffy as an intelligent entity did Tuffy agree to respond. Through the summer of 1964 Miss Duffield spent every available evening and weekend working with Tuffy until finally she established a rapport.

At the time this happened no one was aware that an extraordinary precedent had occurred, and I suspect that the empathy and essential response that was built between Miss Duffield and this particular irascible dolphin has yet to be seen in its full light. Certainly this vital first accord has been eclipsed by the feats Tuffy would achieve as a result of his "taming" by Miss Duffield. Before we move on to these achievements it is worth noting that a few years in the future another woman, Margaret Howe, would live and work with another bottle-nosed dolphin, Peter, and also establish an extraordinary empathy—a level of understanding that would cause the doyen of dolphin research, John Cunningham Lilly, to radically alter his approach to dolphins.

Not all of Tuffy's changed attitude to his human associates

was ignored, however, and Dr. Ridgeway decided that Tuffy could be used for a series of tests which would investigate some of the questions asked at the start of this chapter. How was it that this air-breathing mammal so close to man in so many other ways could apparently move through the sea with apparent immunity to the problems of depth, pressure, bends, narcosis, embolism that so plagued his cousin, man? Or more specifically, how deep could Tuffy, now an interested participant willingly following a boat into the deep ocean, dive without ill effect?

We must now consider two realities of diving which will be known to my fellow scuba addicts. You can make two kinds of dives. One is called a bounce (or no-stop) dive. This means going down and coming up without a long pause in which the nitrogen in the blood can become a deadly bubble. Such dives are of limited duration according to how deep you go. At a depth below 100 feet, the time limit becomes so short—a matter of a few minutes on the bottom—as to render the dive hardly worth the trouble. Normally any dive to what for man is deep requires a decompression stop on the way up to allow the nitrogen to convert itself back into a harmless blood component.

Man's knowledge of where and when the problems of gas bubbles, called "the bends," occur is still primitive. There are stories of bends (they can result in "rotting" of bone joints) happening on a dive no deeper than 30 feet. The most bizarre aspect of this phenomenon is that you may suffer bends after leaving the water. During my extended diving expedition in the Azores we realized we had been subjecting ourselves to considerable risk by driving over a 1,000-foot pass to a new location after a series of dives.

With Tuffy's willing help, Sam Ridgeway set out to establish whether dolphins suffered the same problems, and if not, why.

By now Tuffy had reached a unique level of cooperation probably unmatched in human/dolphin history, and this single fact may well account for the remarkable results Ridgeway achieved. His test equipment was simple in design but complicated in effect. He was out to establish how deep Tuffy could bounce-dive (without any pause for decompression) but, more important, what was different about the dolphin's metabolism which would allow deep dives. The test equipment had to achieve three purposes: show the depth of the dive, to see what was happening physically to Tuffy at depth and to reveal somehow what had happened inside Tuffy during the dive.

Ridgeway decided he would ask Tuffy to dive very deep—to the end of a line lowered several hundred feet beneath his boat; to take a photograph of himself with a camera attached to the end of the line; to come up without stopping; and to breathe out into a collecting device that would allow Ridgeway to study the final contents of his lungs!

I cannot actually recall when I became finally convinced that dolphins were on a par with man but it is certainly true to say that when I first read of these complex demands Ridgeway made of Tuffy—and they took place some years ago—they spelled the end of any lingering doubts.

Needless to say, Tuffy amicably performed all these tasks and Ridgeway got his facts—a set of very startling facts!

The photographs of Tuffy at depth showed that the dolphin had literally changed his shape—the rib cage having hinged inward to assist with the control of the air content of the lungs. At great depths, air, remember, becomes a dangerous, if essential, gas, and the less you have in your lungs the better.

Studies of Tuffy's exhaled breath—he breathed out into a large funnel attached to the side of Ridgeway's boat; studies which were later expanded by Scronce, Kanwisher and Scholander—showed that the dolphin underwater was doing things with air that man has no hope of achieving.

There was a relative insensitivity to carbon dioxide. During a dive the distribution of oxygen was being "controlled" vascularly, with priority going to the brain and heart. Organs least likely to be affected by a lack of oxygen, such as the muscles, were left to work anaerobically. The dolphin's general metabolism seemed to be capable of incurring an "oxygen debt" without damage, which could be paid off later. The blood itself had a high oxygen capacity, and oxygen could be stored in muscle myoglobin other than in the lungs. That dolphins could hold their breath longer than man was taken for granted. Tuffy held his for nearly five minutes on one dive; another record exceeds seven minutes.

But it was the depths of the bounce dives that surprised everyone. Ridgeway lowered his test line even deeper into the water and Tuffy happily followed it, until finally he made an extraordinary plunge to 1,000 feet—without any ill effects!

When Sam Ridgeway trailed Tuffy home that day he knew he was dealing with an animal that lived in a dimension well outside the range of man. But Tuffy was only just beginning his career.

While Ridgeway was working with Tuffy, Sealab Two with three teams of "aquanauts" was being lowered into 205 feet of water off La Jolla for man's first attempt at living on the sea bottom.

This was deadly deep. The teams went into what is called "saturation," a technique for extended deep diving which involves breathing almost pure helium. "The atmosphere in the living compartment contained approximately 85 percent helium, 11 percent nitrogen and 4 percent oxygen, at approximately 103 p.s.i.," the official report states.

Pressure existed as a constant hazard and involved a custom-built set of expensive hardware, again well illustrated by the official report:

> The at-sea decompression of ten divers saturated at a depth of approximately 200 feet presented a new problem for the U.S. Navy. First, the men would have to be lifted from the ocean floor in a Personnel Transfer Capsule maintaining the ocean-floor pressure to the surface-support vessel. Second, they must be transferred to a larger, more comfortable deck decompression chamber, where they undergo lengthy decompression.

Visibility outside Sealab was never more than 30 feet and more often no more than 5 feet. The temperature of the water was a chilly 48°F. In summary, the divers had relative safety inside the steel tube that was Sealab Two—outside they were as vulnerable as a tortoise without its shell. Communicating with the aquanauts was totally dependent on tenuous radio links. Servicing their habitat was as lengthy a business as getting the men there in the first place, and emergency help was available only from other "saturated" aquanauts who had their hands pretty full anyway.

Enter Tuffy! Word had leaked out of Ridgeway's experiments, but it seems the officials were more than a little wary of what seemed incredible claims both of diving ability and trainability, because Tuffy's invitation to join the Navy and become an aquanaut was at first "unofficial"—meaning that he would not be paid for by the Sealab project.

But Ridgeway eagerly grabbed the opportunity to extend the scope of his star pupil and Tuffy was flown to La Jolla, where he proceeded, literally and figuratively, to run rings around his human colleagues.

The dolphin became, through his immunity to pressure problems, Sealab's mail boy, flashing up and down to the submerged capsule with consummate ease. He went on to become an assistant mechanic, carrying and retrieving tools from the aquanauts foraying tentatively onto the sea bed in much the same way as their lunar colleagues were later to stumble across the moon.

Then it was decided to try something much more complicated. The rescue problem had always lurked as a primary danger. With such poor visibility, an aquanaut could easily become lost, and the same problem would hamper colleagues who set out to find him. But for Tuffy, fully equipped with dolphin sonar and sharp ears that could hear a buzzer over a great distance, it was no problem at all. Within days he had been trained not just to find a "lost" diver, but first to collect a ring with a rescue line from Sealab and take it out to his subject!

In the event, the huge report of Sealab Two—there were 48 chapters of it—now proudly contains a section entitled "Utilization of Porpoises in the Man in the Sea Program." At the same time it must be admitted that the rest of this costly project can be summed up in a few words: it is almost pointless for man to contemplate a viable sea-bed program with his present technology. And as an extension of that it must be said that only the dolphin and the other cetaceans could do it for us.

The Navy had the sense to realize this. Sealab Three has yet to materialize—but work with dolphins and their larger brothers had achieved a huge boost.

Requests poured in from a whole range of Navy departments for Tuffy's services. The project officer in charge of test launchings of the Regulus missile was losing the reusable cradles used to support these projectiles through liftoff in the muddy waters of the test range. He had gotten through seven cradles worth $5,000 apiece when he heard of Tuffy and asked the Point Mugu team whether their "humanised porpoise" might find them. All it took was the attachment of a suitable buzzer and when the next cradle plopped into the sea, Tuffy was there to locate it. He performed the same service for the Naval Ammunition Depot in Hawaii (by now Tuffy was a hardened jet-setter), where he found a valuable experimental depth charge, and later, off Santa Rosa Island, plowed unperturbed through stormy sea to tag nine drill mines air-dropped during a fleet exercise.

As I said earlier in this chapter, the average depth of the sea is in excess of 12,000 feet, and while Tuffy was unquestionably an outstanding success as a recovery diver, Navy scientists realized that even his extraordinary depth ability was limited in real oceanic terms.

It was known that the dolphin's big brothers—the toothed whales ranging in size from 20-foot pilots right up to the 60-foot sperm whales—could dive much deeper than the small dolphins. If Tuffy was a worthy Navy recruit—and he saved the Navy several hundred thousand dollars in time and hardware during his period in service—could his larger brothers perform the same service on objects lost in deeper waters?

"Project Deep Ops" was conceived in 1968 and Navy buyers went off on what must surely be their most extraordinary errand —returning with Ahab and Ishmael, two of the species *Orcinus orca* that are wrongly named "killer whales," each weighing about 5,000 pounds, and Morgan and Pip, two pilot whales with a weight of 1,200 pounds each.

All four animals were shipped to the newly opened Naval Undersea Research and Development Center, Hawaii, after they had received boat-follow and open-sea training at Point Mugu.

Pip died of a massive lung infection after a year, and two very strange incidents were to occur with the killer whales which we will consider later. These incidents, to my knowledge, have never been reviewed as anything other than aberrant behavior, but new information has come to light recently about the intelligence of killer whales which could throw an entirely new light on the events.

Morgan, the pilot whale, was to outperform even the legendary Tuffy. Like Tuffy, however, he was a slow starter. He seemed afraid of entering the open sea and had to be lured away from the familiar corner of his floating pen. But within twenty-eight days this young animal was not only coming on command to a buzzer but had learned the discipline of butting the sound source and then waiting stationary for the next command.

Two weeks later he had passed what the Navy called "in-water handling" to the degree where he would tow a man hanging on to his dorsal fin to various recall positions (proving at long last that the "boy on a dolphin" stories of the ancient Greeks were not legends).

Morgan learned to follow a boat out into the open sea and even to "plane" on the stern wave to conserve energy on long hauls. Here he contentedly took to wearing a harness with a radio pack.

He learned to carry rings in his mouth and deposit them on a given target, and raised no objection to what the Navy described as "various devices" being attached to the ring.

And finally this graduate cetacean bit down on one of the strangest devices ever designed by man—a kind of giant gum shield to which was attached a pair of huge tongs and a hydrazine lift device.

Handling, or more accurately, mouthing, this piece of hardware was where all Morgan's training had been leading to, and once he became adept, Navy trainers and their star pupil turned for the open ocean.

Dolphin Tuffy, remember, had "worked" to a depth of 1,000 feet. Pilot whale Morgan, loaded down with his grabber, was not only asked to dive deeper but to engage in much more complicated tasks. It was intended that Morgan would not just find torpedoes and warheads but attach his grabber accurately to them—at depths that would reduce any human diver to jelly.

The animal was successful beyond the wildest dreams of his Navy trainers, as this enthusiastic report, in what is otherwise a very clinical record, indicates:

During one extraordinary session in June, when the target was placed in 1,140 feet of water, Morgan made 9 voluntary dives on the target. Also on the 28th July 1971, during a session when the target had been placed at a 2,000 foot depth, he made a free dive of more than 13 minutes, indicating that he probably made it to that depth.

By the end of July his ability with the grabber had also progressed rapidly, and by August the Navy had the satisfaction of seeing their dummy torpedoes suspended on hydrazine-filled bags popping up all over the ocean from depths averaging 1,500 feet and finally 1,654 feet. It should be remembered that these were not just up-and-down dives. Morgan had to get down to these depths, find the torpedo, align himself and his grabber against currents and then get the grabber fixed in place. Not only did he achieve these complicated exercises but he also appeared to care. There is a piece of film of Morgan "fiddling" with a grabber that he had successfully attached. The hydrazine lifter had failed to activate and Morgan was apparently trying to nudge the device to get it to operate!

So much for the star—what happened to the chorus? Pip, as we have noted, died. The two killer whales quit!

Navy propaganda plays down these defections—the star of the official Deep Ops film is Morgan—but the Deep Ops report goes into the matter in more detail. To my knowledge, researchers who have analyzed the Deep Ops project have always followed the official line and stayed with Morgan. I would briefly like to follow the killer whales because I believe their behavior may well indicate levels of intelligence that have been overlooked but could be as important as the "success" of Morgan. This theory is supported by much new evidence on the remarkable intelligence of killer whales.

Ishmael and Ahab both passed their early exams and progressed right up to the use of the mouth-held grabber—a very complex process of learning, as we have seen.

Ishmael was the first of the killer whales to quit, but not before he had done what the Navy were asking of him. In February he took the grabber and made a dive to 500 feet. His trainers asked him to go on. After the third command he surfaced, spat out the grabber and (I quote from the official report) "lop-tailed (kicked his tail) and slapped his pectoral fins in apparent anger and frustration." A few minutes later Ishmael turned his back on his human companions and the free food of several months and ran for the open sea.

Ahab continued to cooperate for another four months. He successfully deployed the grabber on lost torpedoes as deep as 850 feet. But on June 8—after three practice dives—he went off on his own for a swim. The official record again: "Through the next 14½ hours he would answer the recall and follow the boat only if the crew's plans followed his." Or put another way—I've played your games for six months, now we play mine!

Ahab took his trainers for a ride for a total of 24 hours—a very rough ride in that wave heights were between 6 and 12 feet—then he swam home for dinner. The battered Navy crew had had enough: "Thereafter dive training sessions were terminated with Ahab."

Elsewhere in this book it will be demonstrated that boredom and frustration occur frequently with the larger-brained cetaceans. Killer whales have been noted for their intelligence since the turn of the century when Robert Scott, of Antarctic fame, recorded a very famous encounter in his diary of the fated last expedition.

Scott noted six or seven killer whales skirting the ice into which the bow of his ship was locked. Out on the ice two sled dogs were tied to the bow rope. Standing nearby was an expedition member, Ponting. As Scott watched the pack of whales lifted out of the water and spotted the dogs. Ponting ran toward them to photograph the whales. "The next moment the whole flow under him and the dogs heaved up and split into fragments. One could hear the booming noise as the whales rose under the ice and struck it with their backs. Whale after whale rose under the ice, setting it rocking fiercely."

By chance, neither Ponting nor the dogs lost their footing on the heaving shards. The whales reared out of the water "to a height of six to eight feet" and Scott commented, "There cannot be a doubt that they looked up to see what had happened to Ponting and the dogs."

If you break down this account you end up with an extraordinary set of "intelligent" actions.

- A pack of killer whales spot a food target.
- They decide on a group attack.
- They work out a complicated tactic—breaking the ice under the target.
- They communicate the decided attack and the exact target to other members of their group.
- The attack is signaled and pressed home by the group.
- Everyone surfaces to judge their success.

I believe that what we see in the "failure" of the Deep Ops killer whales is the reaction of an extremely intelligent species to a game that had grown "frustrating" in its pointlessness. As such it is a better pointer to intelligence than the docile and doglike behavior which was the basis of Morgan's success. As it happens, pilot whales have since been shown to have considerably smaller brains than killer whales.

No matter—by the close of the Sealab, Quickfind and Deep Ops programs, the dolphins, big and small, had revealed to man many of the secrets of their absolute adaptation to the sea. The evidence of a sublime species was building rapidly.

FIVE

Second Sight

HOW did the dolphin workmates of the Sealab team find the lost divers in the stygian darkness of the deep ocean?

Long before this first tentative attempt by man to live on the bed of the sea, we had suspected that dolphins possessed an extra dimension of "vision." How it worked, or even what it was exactly, remained a mystery that eluded the researchers until a mere twenty years ago. All we had to work on before that was the observations of fishermen who had noted that dolphins could not only find fish in murky waters and at night, but also seemed able to avoid the fine nets which the fishermen cast around the dolphin's prey.

More astute seafaring folk also noted that there had never been an instance of a dolphin colliding with anything even though these animals moved blithely and at great speed in conditions of negative visibility. The pilot whale acquired his name from grateful navigators who learned to rely on this species of dolphin for a safe passage through rock-strewn waters, passages that were often made at night or in dense fog.

By the beginning of the '50s the military motivation, as we have seen, began to exert its influence, and this seemingly magical sense was set on a par with the dolphin's hydrodynamics as a feature which atavistic man could use.

A description of Russian research in this area summarizes somewhat ominously (if with more honesty than can be found in the West) the prime purpose of the intensive wave of research both superpowers were soon to embark upon: "Bioacoustics . . . are being investigated with the aim of improving means of communication, of finding ways of setting up informational contact with animals and of controlling their behavior."

The first breakthrough came in America when Woods indicated for the rest of the world the right place to look. It was nothing to do with vision as we know it, in which images come via the eyes. In 1954, F. G. Woods made a list of the "sounds" made by dolphins and it was quickly realized, even though his recordings were inadequate, that these sounds might be the equivalent of something of which man already had a rudimentary knowledge—sonar, or as it used to be called in Britain, asdic (Anti Submarine Detection Investigation Committee). Sonar or asdic systems send out a pulse of sound—a ping. If the ping hits anything it bounces back to the sender, and as it travels at a known speed, the returning signal can be measured and a judgment made of the distance of the target object. Throw out a band of pings and you can make a judgment of the shape of the object.

The significance of Wood's dolphin sound recordings was picked up quickly by other scientists, and by 1956 W. E. Schevill and B. Laurence had improved the quality of recording apparatus by using better underwater receivers, called hydrophones, and were able to show conclusively that dolphins were using pings—sonar—to locate fish in muddy waters where it would be impossible for them to use their eyes.

They did not realize, however, that this was a Pandora's box within a box—that the structure of sounds emitted by dolphins with echo location in mind was to prove so complex and delicate as to present man with an entirely new concept of vision and communication.

As had happened with the cracking of Gray's Paradox, the ever-obliging dolphin was again asked to cooperate in bizarre human games in the name of science, games which proved an even greater vindication of Plutarch's accolade of disinterested friendship.

Dolphins were temporarily blinded by means of rubber suction cups and sent to retrieve objects. They were asked to desist from eating their fish and judge their sizes; to choose one species of fish from another.

From 1958 to 1962, one of America's most distinguished dolphin researchers, W. N. Kellog, set dolphins a series of sonar tests so complex as to almost appear to be a test of Dr. Kellog's creative imagination rather than of a dolphin's echolocating powers. Even when his test animal was asked to choose a dinner tantalizingly cut off behind a sheet of transparent glass from a free-floating snack, the dolphin (who I hasten to add was later well fed for his forbearance and restraint) did so accurately and without complaint.

Not to be outdone in the matter of culinary control, Norris spent a good part of 1967 making fake fish out of water-filled gelatin capsules and asked his dolphin to sort them from real fish of identical size. The dolphin sorted them.

Echolocation had become the "in" field of dolphin research as man entered the '60s. It is almost impossible to present an accurate chronology, or specifically credit who did what and when over the next ten years. K. S. Norris set dolphins to judge metal spheres according to their diameter, W. E. Evans had them selecting copper plates from aluminum ones, while Kellog, R. Busnel and S. Dziedzic were competing with their dolphins in a series of obstacle races—through metal rods, nylon cord, thin wire, pipes and nets. And these are the best-known front runners. In France, Britain, Scandinavia, Japan and the Soviet Union others less well known were probing the dolphin's ability to see with sound. If I left anyone out, as indeed I must, an apology. In any event the researchers who have been and will be credited made use of their colleagues' findings and the knowledge we have today is nothing but the sum of a great deal of dedicated work.

But now it is time John Cunningham Lilly, whose name has cropped up previously in this account, is properly introduced, as it is at this point in the late '50s that Dr. Lilly began the work, much of it on sound, that I believe should accord him the title of father of contemporary dolphin research.

It is not so much that his work exceeds in weight (although a total count might well add up to that) the research projects of other famous dolphin pioneers like Kellog and Norris. Lilly's unique place in the field stems, in my considered opinion, from the fact that he opened his mind to the true potential of dolphins and was prepared to explore the physical in tandem with the metaphysical from the very beginning and has never wavered from that course.

In terms of reputation, this has not been without cost. I first met Dr. Lilly at a house which hangs close against the sky at the elevated end of Dekker Canyon off Malibu Beach in California. This meeting I approached with some considerable timidity, not to say temerity, in that I had that same year explored some of the more obvious mysteries of dolphins in a film shown on television. I knew that Lilly was ferociously well qualified with a bachelor of science degree from the California Institute of Technology, laid on top of a medical doctorate from Pennsylvania. I had read his pioneer work on dolphins, *Dolphins and Man*, and had, in company with many others, experienced an extraordinary awakening of wonder on reading his later classic *The Mind of the Dolphin.* And of course I was aware of his famous dolphin-research establishment at St. Thomas in the U.S. Virgin Islands, where a dolphin made the first sounds that could in any way be related to the spoken English language. I had seen both Dr. Lilly and the dolphin suffer a gruesome commercial parody by George C. Scott (surely accidental) and a dolphin with a dubbed neohuman voice in the feature film *The Day of the Dolphin.*

But the truth of the matter is that I had not seen fit to consult Lilly in any form for my own film project even though it represented itself as an up-to-date report on the status of dolphin research, and this, in terms of what I know of the man now, was gross and inexcusable negligence.

I did have a reason, and I think it is time this reason was aired both in the interests of Dr. Lilly's reputation and in support of some of the suggestions I have made about the peculiar mental cataracts which seem to grow over the visionary senses of clinical scientists at a rate somehow equatable with the growth of their reputations.

By the middle of the '60s, John Lilly's fame and reputation had soared like a fiesta rocket, but for the reasons which make him unique, he remained a man of vision. Rather than entrenching what till then had been orthodox, if astonishing, studies of dolphins and proceeding step by methodical step along a clinical road which would eventually have led to that point which caused Johnson to comment acidly, "A scientist is a person who proves nothing until there is nothing left to prove" (or words to that effect), Lilly brought himself to a halt.

He sat back and allowed the wider potential of all he had learned about dolphins to invade his mind. The word "invade" is chosen advisedly, for the opening of this floodgate resulted in something close to mental chaos, or at least that is how I would describe the mazes of awareness, experiments with perception, guilt and confusion as to his own morality and the rights *Homo sapiens* accord themselves, that were to burst out in a series of strangely evocative books with even stranger titles—*The Human Biocomputer, The Center of the Cyclone* and *The Dyadic Cyclone.*

As a writer I suspect these may be textbooks of the future (or at least carefully edited, clarified versions of them) which generations far ahead of ours, generations which will have quantified the embryonic "awareness" that exists among younger people today, will revere.

I have not strayed so far from my point as it may seem. While John Lilly was moving into another dimension, triggered by dolphins and supported by an elite cult of young thinkers (the very existence of this cult made matters worse), traditional science plodded on and viewed his activities with amusement and in some cases open contempt.

When I inquired as to Lilly's current field of work at a time of researching my film, answers varied from "Oh, he's burned himself out" to "He's become very weird" to "The last I heard it was rather sad. Isn't he a drug addict?" This, traditional science's record of a period in which Lilly had written five major books and published an untold number of papers!

So you may imagine the timidity with which I wound my way up Dekker Canyon. This feeling was soon to be replaced by one of relief when John Lilly, a tall, slim man with perceptive gentle eyes, welcomed me with great affection and told me he had climbed all the way up to the top of the canyon with a portable television recorder in order to pick up the best reception of my film.

We (diplomatically on his part, advisedly on mine) did not discuss the content of the film, although he was extremely interested in the detailed check experiments we had conducted at Harderwijk. We found common ground when Lilly expressed considerable pleasure that the film had, for the first time on the mass media, dared to suggest that clinical science was in danger of blindfolding itself on the subject of dolphins. He then proceeded to bury me in piles of papers and manuscripts which showed how he had been making just this point for almost twenty years.

Scanning these works (I remember in particular a piece entitled "The Rights of Cetaceans under Human Law," which was in no sense satirical), it became fairly clear why the upper hierarchy of traditional science had committed John Lilly to a partial state of Coventry. The reports I had heard, considered in the context of the reports I was reading, evoked distinct echoes of another animal scientist who had been forced to travel in limbo when he produced evidence to suggest that man is something less than sublime. I refer, of course, to Charles Darwin.

I plan to deal in some depth with Lilly's work in the chapters to come, not just because I believe he has been wronged (I must stress that the man himself would regard this as an exaggeration) but, more important, because when it comes to the subject of the minds of men and dolphins (and it will be seen that an understanding of one is inevitably interlocked with an understanding of the other), John Lilly has no peer.

But for the time being we must go back to the '50s to a holiday beach on an idyllic island, to a chalet which was the first complete home to be built by man for dolphins and where, a few years later, a dolphin was to fall in love with a young woman and say sweet nothings to her. It began as a very clinical exercise. And to understand that exercise we must first do a little science homework.

The time has come to say something about the nature of sound. The '60s were a good time for sound. A new wave of rock bands were bending our ears from coast to coast, and children who, before this time, had regarded listening as something their parents did, began to vibrate, literally, to a series—a very loud series—of waves that came at them invisibly through the air, shook their livers, lungs and baby brains until vibration became mistaken for emotion—and they screamed!

What was this invisible force that had the kids falling about in the aisles? It was pressure, fluctuation through a flexible medium (for us air, for dolphins water) at a variety of speeds, called wavelengths. To imagine a wavelength, imagine the ocean —the wavelength of a sound is the distance between wave peaks. Now plant a buoy in the ocean and count the number of wave peaks that pound past every second. If they were sound waves your count would be their frequency. A German physicist, Hertz, did the pioneer work on wave counting and the unit of frequency is called the hertz (abbreviated to Hz) after him. One Hz equals one wave (sometimes called a cycle) per second.

If you were ever at a rock concert you will be aware that sound waves come thick and fast, so in the counting of sound waves a multiple of a thousand (kilo) is often added and frequencies commonly counted by kilohertz or kHz. To relate this mumbo-jumbo to something one can actually hear, imagine a quick ripple on the piano. The lowest note you heard had a frequency of about 27 Hz; the high one down the right-hand end of the keyboard just over 4,000 Hz (4 kHz).

In 1959, John Lilly turned aside from prestigious work in neurophysiology to commit himself to a full-time study of dolphins and, perhaps more significant, to find a place where dolphins could be studied full-time. A small part of his funding came from the National Science Foundation in cooperation with the Office of Naval Research and the Department of Defense, and, as was admitted much later, he had been given the world's most bizarre brief. The Communications Research Institute of St. Thomas, as it was later called, had a secondary purpose. Lilly had been asked to investigate how we might talk to aliens in space!

Today we live an age of space detritus mentally and physically; we have walked on the moon and achieved nothing but the destruction of fantasies. We have circled Mars and studied the pockmarked face of Venus and discovered nothing—or nothing at least which will cause the public to allow interruptions of TV football in favor of silver blobs in lunar dust. Our only real discovery has been that our fears of cosmic loneliness, at least in terms of near space, are valid. There never was a man on the moon, and the rest is so far away as to be tomorrow's fantasy. We have come down to earth, and the grand excitement, the great space adventure of the '60s, has been reduced to an invisible junkyard of dying satellites.

When John Lilly went to St. Thomas, there was still the possibility that those silver blobs might need to talk to green blobs! And of course there is still that chance today, although, God help us, it had better be soon, because Lilly is our only trained interpreter and he is no longer as young as he was.

He chose dolphins because they were the nearest aliens from another world. His choice of a place and a facility for study was an early warning of how Lilly would think about dolphins. It was a place where, in his own words, "dolphins could take a good look at the human race."

But I must not allow myself to be drawn down that avenue—not yet, anyway.

On a point facing the trade winds they built a ramp to steal waves; water which tumbled constantly out of the ocean into a pool 70 feet long, 20 feet wide and 10 feet deep. The laboratory was built partly over this pool, with an elevator carrying a water box in which a dolphin could travel in comfort from the pool to the laboratory. Alongside the laboratory was built an electronics room, and most of the first floor was taken up with facilities for analyzing sound. Step one in talking to aliens is to listen to them.

The St. Thomas Island facility began recording what were to become miles upon miles of tapes with the best equipment then available to man. At the end of the first sequence of tests it was recognized that the problems were infinitely more complex than they had ever anticipated.

As a start, their advanced equipment revealed that the dolphin was making many more sounds than had been expected. After several months of careful checking, Lilly split these sounds into four main categories: whistles; sonic clicks (clicks we could hear); ultrasonic clicks (clicks outside our hearing ability); and rapid click trains with various characteristics.

Later he was to add another category—"A class of sounds that are Humanoid"—but we will hear more of that in a later chapter.

Starting with the whistles, the researchers were soon facing the fact that the dolphins' hearing-frequency spectrum was *five times* as broad as ours. Allied research on one aspect of the dolphin's brain showed that on the ear side dolphins possessed two and a half times as many major connection fibers as man.

You may now need to reread that section featuring Mr. Hertz. The St. Thomas Island tapes revealed that the dolphin rarely transmitted signals much below a frequency of 6 kHz. Referring back to our run on the piano, the highest note played was 4 kHz. Or more simply, dolphins would like Maria Callas but would hate Paul Robeson, if they were capable of hate.

What they liked most of all were sounds we could not even hear. They were comfortable at 24 kHz and could soar to a super-soprano scream peaking at about 170 kHz.

And that was just the whistling! When Lilly and his colleagues turned to the clicks—and we are now back to where this chapter should be—we were truly in another dimension of sound, a conception that was to start as a piece of mathematics but, as its potential and scope was realized, would be recognized as a new dimension of vision.

The clicks were going out at frequencies as high as 300 kHz.

That was the high clicks. There were also clicks we could hear (not as clicks, admittedly; the bursts were too fast and we heard them as "creaks").

Then, and I suspect this must have been a moment approaching hysteria on that otherwise idyllic island, Lilly and Co. discovered that the dolphins could whistle and click together, whistle in the sonic and click in the ultrasonic at the same time, or (or perhaps and/or) click in the sonic and the ultrasonic at the same time—in fact they could even operate each side of their bodies independently and use each of their two sound-making mechanisms separately; one to have a companionable whistle at a nearby lady dolphin, the other to give her a quick sonar once-over. All this from the same head!

These discoveries were made when the team stopped listening (and one can have considerable sympathy) and started looking at how the dolphin created this marine babel.

Dolphins breathe through holes in the tops of their heads—if you like, "nostrils" similar to ours which evolution has moved back to the most convenient position for an animal which has to surface to breathe. At first glance there is apparently only one blowhole, but this splits into two channels and at the base of these channels the dolphin has its phonation mechanism.

That other grand figure of dolphin research, Kenneth Norris, has shown, using X-ray pictures, that the dolphin makes his sonar clicks by vibrating the tough muscular plugs which the animal also uses to close his "nostrils" against water. There is also a theory that the nasal canals may have phonation mechanisms that pinch air into sound waves.

To this day, no one knows for sure how the dolphin makes all its various sounds, although Lilly has speculated that the dolphin's larynx, which does not have what would normally be identified as vocal cords, might be producing some sounds.

Lilly was questioned on this by a man we have already met, Dr. Peter Purves of the British Natural History Museum, at a conference in the U.S. Purves, an anatomist, had accused the largely American conference of "completely neglecting the larynx." But, he pointed out, the larynx was an extremely complex organ in dolphins—"with careful dissection one can show that there are noisemaking mechanisms there too."

Lilly replied that he agreed completely. He reminded his audience of the St. Thomas Island findings that dolphins could emit ultrasonic clicks simultaneously with other sounds and under independent control and that the ultrasonic beam could be turned off and on independently of the sonic wave and the whistles. "There must be a third sound emitter somewhere," Lilly pointed out. "And the larynx is my candidate for the ultrasound."

Another speaker told the conference that the Lockheed research facility had conducted tests in which air was blown through an excised larynx. Adjustments of the arytenoid cartilage had produced whistles very similar to those produced by dolphins. And there, so far as I know, is where it rests. The dolphin has at least two "voices," and more probably three.

Accept, of course, that one of these voices is not a voice—it is an extra pair of "eyes" capable of three-dimensional vision.

So let us stop thinking of the dolphin's clicks as sounds and try to start to see them instead as a method of viewing, a method which we do not possess. Sonar research was, in a major sense, a turning point for dolphin and man. Up until that time our knowledge of the animal had maintained an approximate equality. His body was a marvelous adaption to the sea, but ours wasn't that bad on land, and our cunning little hands had built motorized shells which bowled us along much faster than our inadequate legs. Others took us aloft in spite of our absence of wings or sufficient muscle to flap wings.

But when the full potential of the dolphin's sonar system was recognized, the dolphin began to leave us behind. He possessed an ability, a vision, which existed nowhere in the human race, other perhaps than as a faint echo in blind people, some of whom experience a phenomenon called "shadow vision." But the dolphin was seeing a lot more than shadows.

I want to convert a burst of dolphin clicks to a handful of Ping-Pong balls fired by one of those appalling guns which uncles, who don't like their brothers, give their nephews at

Christmas. Ignore those relationships; stay with the Ping-Pong balls. If you were to arm yourself with one of these devices, position yourself blindfolded in front of a garage door you have never seen, and fire off balls a foot apart in a steady arc, you would instantly learn a lot more than you would believe possible simply from the sounds you heard.

- The width of the garage door
- Its composition, say metal or wood
- Where the door ended and the brick abutment started
- How high the door was
- Whether the door was open or closed
- Whether one was open and the other closed
- If there was anything between you and the door
- Whether that object was moving or stationary

Eight points of information from as many Ping-Pong balls.

If you did a little more preparation, such as working out the speed in feet per second that the gun was throwing the balls, your information retrieval would escalate to a point where you would be getting almost as much as you would without the blindfold. You would know how far away all these different surfaces were.

If you listened a little harder, and practiced on a few more surfaces, and remembered the sounds made by the ball on these surfaces, you could tell whether your door was painted, or where the paint had chipped, and so on.

That is dolphin sonar at its most primitive. But I must stress *primitive*!

Dolphins throw out more than a thousand "Ping-Pong balls" a second, each ball a seeker of complex information serviced by a brain that has spent the last fifty million years developing memory facilities that are beyond our comprehension.

Dolphins can vary the rate at which they click, vary the frequency of the click and vary the range of the signal. They can flatten, shorten or stretch their beam of clicks, and although they normally push these beams out directly in front of them, they can also transmit them sideways.

The dolphin focuses these beams by projecting the sounds out of the head down the longitudinal central axis of the skull, "pointing" them as required by building the maximum acoustic pressure at the point of the beak (rostrum). It has also been suggested that the adipose (fatty) cushion on the forehead of dolphins helps this focusing in that this tissue is a better transmitter of sound waves than other body tissue, or, for that matter, water.

There is no way my Ping-Pong analogy can stretch to encompass this, so instead we will travel again to the Dutch research establishment at Harderwijk, where I was able to watch C. Kamminga, from the Laboratory of Information Theory, Delft University, make his own, and I believe most recent, attempt to check just how finite is the dolphin's ability to collect information by sound pulsing.

What the Dutch researchers set themselves, and a dolphin called Doris, to do was in fact a test of the whole team. Doris was asked to confirm all that had been gathered about dolphin sonar up till then, add a few new items of information such as how the sonar beam was being focused and, with the researchers using more sophisticated equipment, provide sounds for them to analyze. The researchers were out to test themselves by devising the most complex sonar equipment they could think of.

The test looked extremely simple—two black balls hanging on the ends of wires. Doris was not hampered by complex equipment—she had a sensitive hydrophone trailing a thin wire stuck on her rostrum by a suction cup.

In fact the two black balls were not simple at all. They were virtually identical. They were both black, made of aluminum and machined so accurately that a micrometer showed no difference. Doris was set the task of "weighing" them using her sonar, because one of the balls was slightly hollow, and therefore lighter.

How can a dolphin weigh an object without the aid of scales, without touching it? By sound.

Doris, who finally ran the test 960 times (in passing, an

interesting test of her good nature), "weighed" the balls (she had been trained to indicate the hollow ball every time they were swung round) with an accuracy rate of 92 percent!

This time the phenomenon was not left as another dolphin "wonder." The microphone on her beak and the ultrasensitive equipment used to record the sounds she was bouncing off the spheres gave the researchers the answers. Mr. Kamminga explains:

> We were able to record and in fact photograph from an oscilloscope that the dolphin had to be reading not one but several echoes coming back from the spheres.
>
> The first set of echoes returning from the two spheres are identical and at first we were puzzled as to how Doris was successfully choosing the hollow sphere. Then we realized that there is a small difference in time between the first and second echo in both cases.

It took some very hard study of the echo patterns to spot this difference. "It is a very slight difference, not a small fraction but a fraction of millionths. Nevertheless it seems the dolphin is capable of reading this difference and separating one sphere from another."

Mr. Kamminga's phrase "fraction of millionths" explains why the Dutch team ran so many tests. It was many months before they were sure enough of themselves to announce that the secondary-echo time lapse from the slightly hollow sphere compared with the solid sphere was three millionths of a second!

An echolocating ability of this sophistication is not a listening device but a new concept in vision which almost transcends the imagination. As I sat at Harderwijk and watched Doris slowly shaking her head (to spread the beam) and then inexorably homing in on the hollow sphere before swinging away to indicate that she had finished her chore, I tended to forget that the balls were identical—identical to me at least. The shifting silver-blue of the water playing on the matt-black sphere caused fluctuating patterns, and my mind became convinced that there must be some visual difference.

But there wasn't.

Doris was actually "looking" *inside* those spheres, and as my mind expanded that concept I felt a mental twinge akin to panic. If I were to stand in the water before a meal, could she see that I was hungry? Yes. If I were to hold a gun behind my back, could she see it? Yes. Could dolphins in the sea look inside ships? Yes. Could they judge the shapes of men, of guns, of cargoes? Yes. And they could judge textures, and shapes, and quantities, and densities, those to the front, and those to the side. . . .

It is an irrational fear because the dolphin has no such motivation yet. And "yet" is the important word, because dolphins learn extremely quickly and have extraordinary memories. This fact emerged as an intriguing bonus for the Harderwijk researchers. Two years after their first test runs, Kamminga brought Doris back to her pool, fitted her hydrophone, lowered the black balls into the water and waited.

In his own words: "It was amazing, it was really amazing. Astonishing! We knew nothing about how she would behave but after a few training runs everything was as before. She stayed with the hollow sphere exactly as she had been taught."

I will leave you to do your own vicarious projections of the things dolphins could be taught (indeed, what they may well be being taught) while I move on to another extension of sonar ability, or more accurately, an application of it.

Can a dolphin read another dolphin's sonar signal; can they share their information; is it possible that there could be an oceanwide net of dolphins in contact? In a later chapter we will consider "talking," but while we are here it is worth examining what is known of range and sonar interchange, because this possibility for me at least must surely be in the realm of science fiction. Perhaps not. The facts favor Contact, with a big C.

Returning to the rock bands for a moment, it is obvious that sound is a good traveler. Draw the blinds and you will cut out the street lamp outside the window, but you will not lose the traffic noise. It is now known that dolphins make sounds that theoretically could travel almost infinite distances, and that on the other hand they can and do produce high-frequency sounds that collect detailed information from objects only short distances away. So range is no problem; theoretically a school of dolphins could read the echolocating pulses of others. Basically, distance is no problem, as dolphins make sounds that can travel great distances—the theoretical range of a 20 Hz sound in a homogeneous sphere of water of even pressure and temperature without reflective surfaces (this is an example for demonstration only) is 21,000 miles. Nor for that matter is time a problem. It would be four times as fast as any vocal exchange we could make on land because sound travels at 4,700 feet per second in water and at a laggardly 1,130 feet per second on land at sea level.

And there we must leave it as an intriguing, or, if you like, frightening dimension that only the dolphins know. Or at least there I thought I would have to leave it until I visited Dr. Lilly and began to work my way through the vast pile of research reports from his work in the Virgin Islands.

On the fourth page of a paper read to the American Philosophical Society in April 1962, Lilly, dealing otherwise with a detailed description of all the various sounds he had heard dolphins make, abruptly injects the following extraordinary nugget:

> The ultrasonic pulses can be locked in or not locked in with sonic pulses. When the sonic pulses are associated with the ultrasonic, they are apparently being used to communicate the sonar information to the nearby animals by means of the lower communication (sonic) band of frequencies.

And then, without comment, he goes on to give a catalog of dolphin sounds.

If Lilly is right in his conclusions (and I have not seen them mentioned, or elaborated, in any other document), then my science-fiction concept of dolphins in contact, not to mention a concept of sharing that comes close to the philosophical panacea of all man's ills, the group mind, could be science fact. I literally dare go no further, for if I have not stretched your credulity to the limit I certainly have my own.

Which gets us where? I hope a little awed. For it is an understanding, if necessary, a poetic understanding of dolphin sonar vision in its infinite complexity which begins to transform the dolphin from an intriguing scientific object to the more spiritual example it represents in the minds of some contemporary thinkers.

We are a product of our senses, molded, educated, developed and rounded by the planet to which we were born and on which we now live; worlds we may judge by our ability to smell, see, taste, hear and touch.

The dolphin has something extra—a sixth sense of awesome perception that man does not possess. They are receiving images from a dimension we cannot enter.

The lure of the dolphin expressed in pictures. Curiosity, awareness, intelligence and an obvious desire for contact are reflected in this dolphin's expression and stance.
Credit: Robin Brown

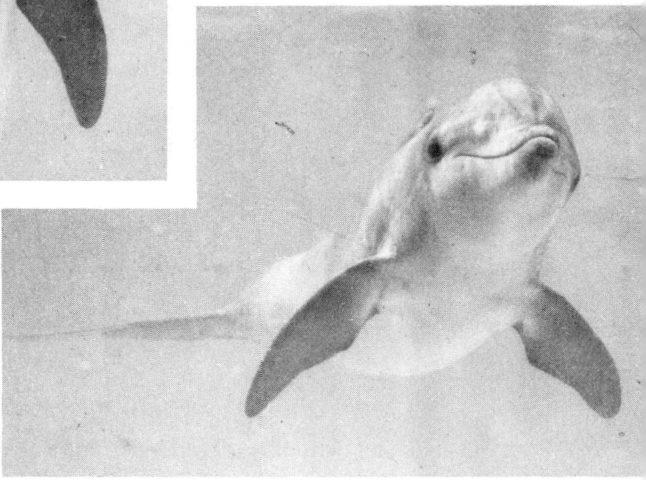

British diver Dr. Horace Dobbs has been involved in a unique friendship with a wild, free dolphin—Donald. Their friendship spans four years and five different meetings. *Credit: Dr. Horace Dobbs*

Dr. Dobbs shows how intimate his contact with Donald has become.

Dr. Dobbs updates a C legend by riding a wild dolphin.

Donald sees himself for the first time in a mirror presented by Dr. Dobbs.

The king of dolphins, Orcinus Orca, misnamed the Killer Whale. Show animals such as this one have revealed to man that the dolphin's legendary goodwill and gentleness apply even to these giants of the family. *Credit: Robin Brown*

Here Orcas are pictured behaving in a way that earned them the name—attacking a giant whale. Recent contact with Orcas, however, reveals that even t seek out a friendly, nonaggressive relationship with man. *Credit: Dolfinarium, Harderwijk, Holland*

A squadron of dolphins rising from the darkness of the deep ocean.

Denizens of the Void. **Seven tenths of the world's surface is covered by water, and dolphins have free use of this massive space. But pictures of dolphins moving freely in their inner universe are rare. This unique set showing dolphins hanging in the void is the work of an intrepid diver, Pat Baker.** *Credit: Pat Baker. Maritime Archaelogical Department, Western Australian Museum*

'lying dolphins. So huge is the space available to dolphins that they appear to fly ather than swim.

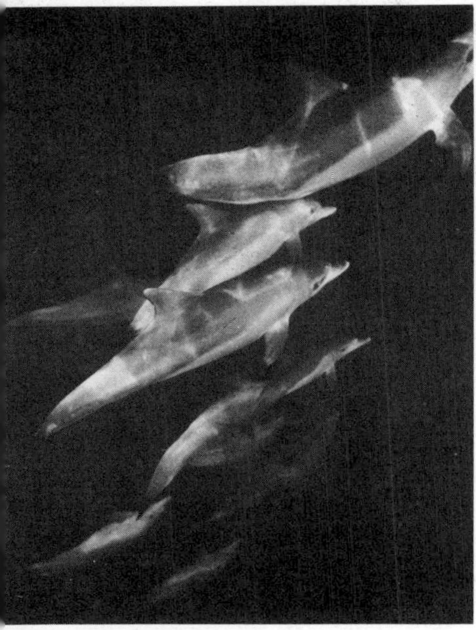

Dolphins at play in the deep ocean. This rare underwater study graphically demonstrates the animal's dexterity in the open ocean: Those in the rear are keeping pace with the foreground dolphins even though they are swimming upside down.

The dolphin's view of human space. Equipped with scuba gear and a motorized underwater camera, Pat Baker threw himself into the wake of a speeding craft to capture this unique view of wild dolphins engaged in their favorite sport of boat following.

f you look behind the lisplays of extraordinary ;ymnastic ability the dol-hin show performed in sea oos throughout the world is n enlightening revelation f the dolphin's ability to hink, plan, communicate nd cooperate. *Credit:)olfinarium, Harderwijk, Iolland*

Dolphins do not normally vocalize in air, but if asked to by man they will produce sounds alone or, as in this case, as a Dolphin Choir. We still have no idea what these sounds mean.

)olphin togetherness. These dolphins engage in complex sound/sonar onversations before leaving the water, hence their perfect meeting in the hoops.

To achieve this degree of perfectic
in formation flying, human aero-
batic teams rely on years of trainir
and on computer assistance.
Dolphins think out a maneuver ar
can bring it to perfection in a
matter of hours.

The only contribution the trainer makes to this coordinated leap is to signal the start. After that the dolphins make their own decisions and moves.

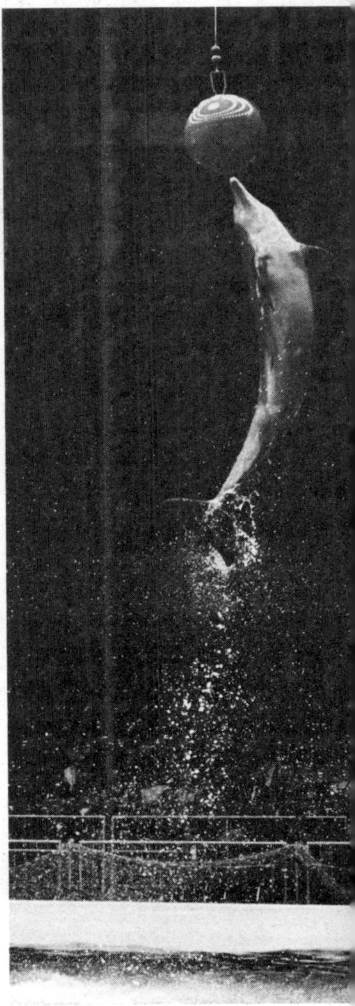

The dolphin is capable of adjusting its eyes for perfect vision both in and out of water, which makes possible such feats of judgment as this power leap to a high ball.

·olphin mothers are strict
ıd seem to have a method
f communicating with
ıeir young that enforces a
ose, coordinated contact
·en when the mother
oves at high speed.
·edit: Walter Bug

Most trainers use a food reward system, but research has shown that dolphins will respond just as well to affection. They get their stimulation from the interest we show in them. *Credit: Dolfinarium, Harderwijk, Holland*

Man's traditional view of the dolphin: a lively, cheeky face lifting from a dolphinarium pool. Intelligence gleams from the eye, but don't be fooled by the grin—it is a genetic accident. *Credit: Leone*

SIX

Speak, Dinosaur!

CHATTERING gabbling man, who uses his voice as much to contain progress as expand it, is incapable of accepting the possibility of real intelligence in another species unless that species can talk.

Unlike any other animals, or so we tell ourselves, we have taken the noises made by our fluctuating throats and coded and disciplined them to a complex form of communication called language.

In the case of most animals, man's claim to higher intelligence is justified, but communication by voice is no kind of exclusive criterion. Brain size, perhaps. Brain complexity coupled with size, certainly. But vocal communication, no. A miming bird is no brighter than a bird that confines itself to birdcalls.

In fact, man has become so enamored with vocal communication we have, if anything, neglected alternative effective methods of communication, almost certainly to our own cost. We assumed that the apes were locked in prehistory by the limitations of their small brains—until committed zoologists like Jane Goodall spent sufficient time studying the apes in their own habitats. We discovered not only that the apes have a complex strata of communication but that they were capable of communicating in our language forms once the right communication equipment had been found; in the case of this particular species, deaf-and-dumb sign language.

But it was in our contact with the dolphin that man's obsession with vocal communication was most dramatically exposed. For a hundred years we had been aware of the dolphin's large and complex brain; for a thousand years mariners had recorded the ability of the whales to communicate warnings of danger; and two thousand years ago the Greeks and Romans had detailed their observations of a sophisticated empathy between dolphins and their young and dolphins and humans.

And yet, in the '60s, when modern science came reluctantly to the conclusion that the dolphin might represent a new peak in the scale of natural intelligences, it turned inexorably to speech as the way of proving it.

If that may seem an excessive condemnation of human myopia, it is worth taking a moment to consider what the researchers were asking of the dolphin when they set out to establish whether they could speak our language. To put it in a nutshell they were asking the dolphin to wind itself back through millions of years of evolution—in effect to speak not English but Dinosaur.

Late chapters in this book will reveal that the dolphin almost certainly does not need our kind of vocal language; that they have a complex, multifaceted communication system which makes the spoken word a very shallow form of contact. There is every reason to believe that the species evolved around language—bypassed it as an inefficient communication method for the world of the sea.

If this is the case, the real nature of the problem we posed for dolphins was as follows, and it requires that I invent a species not yet evolved to project an analogy:

A vast lumbering beast steps through a Time Door built by beings from a world where the atmosphere can be as dense as jelly. Said species—let us call them Nams—once occupied the hot, arid, methane-storm-swept land surface of their world before deciding that the compressed jelly filling the deep valleys offered better protection against the weather and the excess of competing Nams on the limited land surface. To live in the jelly required a number of changes. Talking was a waste of time because the jelly stopped the sound and clogged the throat. Sign language was better but too slow. Telepathy and a complex code of communication based on physical contact were evolved over the new few million years, so that by the time the dinosaur from earth lumbered through the Time Door it found itself confronting a host of perfectly spherical blobs all waving hair-like cilia in perfect rhythm; a rhythm so complex the dinosaur, while frightened and a little nauseated, was forced to conclude the Nams were intelligent.

To the Nams, who had no mouths, no vocal cords, no ears, no arms and no legs, the dinosaur, who had been the superior species on earth for 100 million years, delivered the following edict in a series of thunderous grunts: "Speak to me in Dinosaur and I will accept that you might be my equal."

That, in a science-fiction wrapping, is the edict man delivered to dolphins.

But what is even more extraordinary is that, overcoming immense, almost unimaginable difficulties, the dolphin did learn a little of the English/Dinosaur language. And before we go on to see how that came about it is also worth placing on record that not one of the men and women who engaged in speech experiments with dolphins for nearly twenty years managed to learn one single word of Dolphin.

As this book goes to print, Dr. Lilly will be pressing the button of a computer that has been programmed to convert our language into a form dolphins hopefully can understand, and vice-versa. But as of this moment, in spite of many years of study and thousands of miles of recording tapes, no human has been able to work out, and voice, any sound that would have an understandable meaning for a dolphin.

And yet we still regard ourselves as the superior species!

By the early '60s, Lilly and others had made a start on sorting out the different sounds made by dolphins. They realized that some of them were for echolocation, others for inter-dolphin communication. More simply, dolphins were using certain of their sounds to "talk" to one another.

Researchers like Vincent, Fish and Mowbray, Busnel and

Dziedzic, Caldwell, Perkins, Schevill and Watkins spent a great deal of time listening to the dolphin babel and were finally able to sort dolphin communication signals into two rough groups: whistles, and a more complex group that have been described as "barking, mewing and creaking."

If we recall our lecture on the way certain sounds travel through water, it should come as no surprise to find that the communication signals were all in the lower dolphin frequencies —usually no higher than 50 kHz, thus ensuring effective range.

The majority of these signals were totally incomprehensible and remain so to this day, although, as we shall discuss later, John Lilly has now embarked on the first serious program using the most advanced technology to sort them into a language sequence. Only the more obvious of cries—joy and excitement while playing or copulating and the signals of distress and/or fear—could be labeled. And none of them bore the vaguest resemblance to anything that might be called human, which was not altogether surprising if you consider the totally different environment in which dolphins live and speak.

Tonight, when you take your bath, stick your head in the water and try to talk! I have even tried this exercise 100 feet underwater breathing from an aqualung. The results are bizarre. A strange Mickey Mouse voice squeaks back to you from all around your head. The deeper you go, the higher the squeak.

The reason this happens is that we simply lose our ability to detect the direction of sounds when we are underwater. On land, we hear sounds via our ears. Underwater, instead of these two separate receivers to which the hearing mechanism of our brain is tuned, our whole skull becomes a receiver—because sound underwater keeps on traveling until it hits something solid enough to stop it, and since the density of flesh and that of water are virtually the same, the thing that stops it underwater is the bone of the skull—the whole skull! This does not happen on land because flesh—the flesh of our ears—is a thousand times denser than air, dense enough to stop airborne sounds.

Millions of years back down the evolutionary scale, mammal dolphins realized that fleshy ear flaps were useless in the ocean and began adapting the bone structure of their heads to be sound receivers. Fatty tissue or blubber, with a density less than water, connected one of these receivers, the forehead region, to the inner ear, while the lower jaw was brought in as a second receiver, this connected by air passages to the inner ear.

That is not to say that the dolphin is in any way deficient in hearing. One of the most dramatic tests ever conducted on the dolphin's hearing was Kellog's famous teaspoon of water. When he dropped this minute quantity into a large dolphinarium pool, the test animal immediately spun round and sent echolocating beams in its direction. It has even been suggested that dolphins find the sound of rain on dolphinarium roofs painful and that the construction sounds in a dolphinarium were severe enough to kill an animal in a nearby tank.

So when the research into the dolphin's ability to speak our language got under way in the '60s, the scientists knew full well how difficult a task they were setting the animals. Quite apart from learning a "language," a communications concept which we must presume on known evidence is alien, the animal would have to learn "hearing." As it turned out, he would also have to learn "speaking," and by that I do not mean the manipulation of his sound-making mechanisms to the shape of words (a concept, given the dolphin's apparent sound-muscle dexterity, that would not be too difficult), but a totally new "speaking" formula—the production of sounds, contained to a frequency we could hear, in air.

It may be said that dolphins made the first step toward speaking to us without our really noticing. The Greeks, who first recorded that dolphins made sounds to humans, considered these airborne transmissions to be natural. We followed their example by taking for granted the sounds dolphins made above water in dolphinariums. They were not; the dolphin does not normally transmit in air.

So considering all these facts it would surely be a miracle beyond equal in human learning if a dolphin were to someday rise out of a pool and say "ball," when asked.

It has already happened.

Just this miracle occurred a few years ago to John Lilly at his St. Thomas laboratory. I have personally heard this tape and can vouch for its authenticity. It is very famous now and a great number of skeptics have questioned the dolphin's "voice," "accent," and so on. To me such hairsplitting is farcical. Considering the immense difficulties the dolphin faces, does it really matter if the animal, asked to say "ball," said "all" or "sh-all" or "br-all"?

The fact is, an alien species reached through uncountable layers of incomprehension and produced a sound unquestionably similar to the sound requested.

It had learned to hear a dinosaur, work out what the dinosaur wanted, adjust the mechanics of its phonation mechanism to those of the dinosaur, pitch its sound to a level the dinosaur could hear, and say the word the dinosaur had asked it to say, when the dinosaur wanted.

I am certain that John Lilly realized its true significance, just as some five years earlier he had abandoned a successful career at the National Institute of Mental Health in Bethesda and the appeals of a respected colleague to commit himself to a full-time study of dolphins, and in particular of the ability of dolphins to speak.

Some time prior to the establishment of the full-time facility in St. Thomas, Lilly had conducted a series of experiments on the dolphin brain at a laboratory established at Marine Studios in Miami, one of which had produced an extraordinary result.

Lilly had been probing the dolphin's brain using electrodes. It is a practice which Lilly has long ago abandoned (but still one which Russian scientists are advocating as "indispensable" in an investigation of perception), but ethical or otherwise it was the sounds the dolphin made under the stimulus of electronic probes that was to lure Lilly into a better appreciation of the animals than any man before or since. Of such paradoxes is respect composed! Lilly records:

When I first discovered this effect in 1957, it was in a series of experiments designed for totally different purposes than studying the vocalization. The effects occurred during a study on the brain of the first animal. During the course of these experiments under certain conditions, the animal was emitting very peculiar sounds that we had not heard from any other dolphin. Later, in retrospective analysis of the tapes on which we were recording our information, we heard unmistakable resemblances to the human voice in these emissions from the dolphin.

It was many months before we were able to believe this evidence. From November 1957 until May 1958, we studied the accumulated information from three animals; in May a preliminary announcement of our findings was made. These findings were met with total disbelief on the part of others who had worked with the dolphins. Since then we have accumulated much corroborative evidence, not only bearing out these early findings, but extending the observations into new areas of experience.

These last lines, gently understated, are in fact a description of several years of work by Lilly and his team at the special laboratory he would go on to build in St. Thomas, work which for this writer at least proves conclusively that dolphins have a facility for human languages which will depend on two factors of elucidation—whether man can project himself forward to a meeting halfway and whether the dolphin, who moves already in his own Utopia, can be bothered. For reasons I do not properly understand, the dolphin seems inclined to be bothered.

John Lilly found considerable evidence of this during his years in St. Thomas, and for this reason and also because it is important you make your own judgment of that accumulation of "corroborative evidence" we must travel again to the place where "dolphins could take a good look at the human race."

In the early '60s the St. Thomas Island dolphins cooperated in a series of experiments under varying conditions of confinement. Although the description of these conditions may seem questionable they were never continued to a point of duress.

Condition one was solitary confinement in a small "room." Two was solitary confinement in a large room. Three was a situation where the animal could not see, touch or smell another dolphin but was in sound contact. Four was two free-swimming animals limited to an acoustic exchange. Five was virtual freedom of contact. In the sixth condition, free contact was allowed, with human beings present and intervening.

Conditions one and two had little purpose other than for the recording of sounds. Lilly noted that in these confined conditions sound emissions gradually decreased and confinement had to be limited to short periods.

Sound transmissions perked up as soon as any "dolphin" influence was introduced, even the spoor of another animal. Even in the large-room condition any stimulus, even the introduction of toys, enhanced sound emissions instantly.

Conditions three, four and five produced an immediate, spontaneous vocalization lasting from a few seconds to many minutes. In a twenty-four-hour day there were at least four hours of vocal contact. Under condition five, with space to play or mate, the dolphins communicated or vocalized for periods up to twenty minutes at a stretch.

Under conditions three, four and five John Lilly heard and described for the first time dolphins engaged in "duets." He described them as a "special phenomenon" in which the animals whistled simultaneously, sometimes matching frequencies and time patterns "so exactly that the relatively low-frequency difference between their simultaneous whistles can be heard."

And finally we arrive at condition six, free contact including the presence of a human being—the condition from which Lilly's corroborative evidence was to emerge. At this stage we must leave the clinical observation of laboratory animals and introduce a few personalities, human and dolphin.

There is Lilly himself, hovering over the whole experiment in a state, one suspects from the accounts of this period, of intellectual schizophrenia; half tied to his clinical training by the need to present findings that his financial backers and scientific colleagues would accept—"It was many months before we were able to believe this evidence"—yet partially seduced and not a little confused by "special phenomenon." Then we have three particular dolphins, Lizzie, Peter and Elvar, and a woman assistant, Margaret Howe, who is to make the first attempt by a member of the human race to "be" with a dolphin to the extent that it is physically possible for a land-oriented mammal to so be.

When one reads of the slow, inexorable drawing together of these five mammals from different worlds one becomes subject to a foreboding of disastrous climax—the sense that something momentous in its originality is about to happen; a conjunction so original as to subject it, inevitably, to question, to cynicism and to disbelief. It is an experience that can only happen to those who are participating in it. It will not stand up to appraisal, or clinical discussion.

The chronology of what I regard as our first real *contact* with dolphins runs as follows.

Studies based on physical contact with dolphins had begun before the St. Thomas laboratory was built, using converted space at the Marine Laboratory of the University of Miami. Lilly had moved away from the brain as a direct area of study and was moving toward what he later described as "beginning from the heart and working out."

He was admittedly drawing on certain personal theories that were the product of studies made while wearing his earlier neurophysiological hat. Lilly had subjected himself to a number of "isolation" experiments which involved being suspended in water for long periods. These experiments (since expanded and recorded in books like *Deep Self*) were aimed at the brain, but Lilly had also noted an increase of skin sensitivity and he now theorized that physical—tactile—contact with a dolphin might well be an important factor in the communication equation.

The animal chosen to participate in these exercises (words like "test" and "experiment" become increasingly less accurate) was Elvar, a 7-foot male dolphin weighing 150 pounds.

Elvar had been captured for Lilly by a famous dolphin catcher, Milton Santini, using techniques of handling—gentle stroking—which Lilly believed could relate to his own tactile sensations in water and could indicate that a contact relationship between humans and a dolphin might be the logical next step forward.

Elvar's makeshift pool was tiny by comparison with the facilities that were later built at St. Thomas, but from the day of his arrival he was fed by hand, and he responded positively within a few days to the human team (who included Alice Miller, the co-author of a number of the more important reports) rubbing and stroking him.

The only voices Elvar heard were human voices, and, as Lilly describes it, "his vocalization began to be less 'delphinese' and to break into more humanoid, wordlike, explosive bursts of Donald Duckish quacking." Lilly reinforced Elvar's continuous contact with the human voice by "bugging" the laboratory with a microphone connected to a hydrophone. Elvar heard everything the humans said, even when he was underwater.

Elvar soon began to make noises in air, sounds which one must assume were aimed at his human companions, and among the "quacking" noises were sounds which Lilly felt were very much like primitive words in the human language.

Initially the animal had been transmitting at an extremely high frequency (rarely lower than 1 or 2 kHz) comparable, as Lilly pointed out, to the high-pitched falsetto children use when they first learn to speak. But when the tapes were slowed down to quarter-speed, certain resemblances to human speech were heard.

The first pair of words which the team could definitely identify, again using this slowed-tape technique, followed a poolside session with Alice Miller. Elvar had been squirting her with water (a common dolphin game), and she cried, "Stop it!" sharply, several times. The fifth cry produced an explosive "reply" from Elvar that was so close to "stop it" as to be beyond coincidence or accident.

The team now realized that the speed of the dolphin's "reply" was a factor to be considered. He was responding so instantly these sounds had sometimes been overlooked. By studying the instant response in detail, Lilly and Miller heard "bye-bye" and "morvar"—a high-speed shortening of "more Elvar."

Lilly himself discovered that Elvar was examining each new human voice and attempting to reproduce its different characteristics. Elvar would repeat words that Alice had taught him, like "speak up" and "louder." He would also split words into interesting bits. Lilly taught him to say "water" after a long sequence of "war" and "ter" delivered separately. Elvar put special emphasis on the *r* during this session and Lilly later realized that he and Alice produced their *r*s very differently.

"He does not reproduce a word in a 'tape recorded' fashion or in the fashion of a talking bird. In one's presence he literally analyzed the acoustic components of our words and reproduced various aspects in sequence and separately."

Lilly concluded, after fifty-one days of working with Elvar, "We began to see that by natural methods, without brain-electrode forcing, it may be possible to teach these animals to vocalize so that we may establish communication with them."

But the conditions at the temporary laboratory were far from ideal, and Lilly realized that to make any real progress he would need a facility specifically designed for the job. He began the search which was to end in the Virgin Islands. It is an indication of his commitment (and a fact I had not realized before) that financial support was not immediately forthcoming and Lilly bought the land by selling his personal estate.

As early as April 1960, less than a year after the first experimental pool had been blasted out of the solid rock of what was to be called Point Dolphin, Lilly experienced his first genuine breakthrough with a dolphin and "English" words.

Lizzie, the test animal, was in fragile health, and Lilly had decided to try force-feeding even though it meant he would be late for his own dinner. Someone called to him, "It's six o'clock," sharply and loudly, over the PA system.

This announcement went onto the tapes via the laboratory microphone, as did the sounds Lizzie and her companion, Baby, made at the same time, underwater. Only when these tapes were being studied in another laboratory some time afterward was it realized that Lizzie, in an exchange with Baby at the time of the shout, had "said" something very closely resembling "It's six o'clock."

"But," Lilly adds, "I was first caught by another meaning. It sounded to me like "This is a trick!" with a peculiar hissing accent. Other people have since heard the tape and come to the same conclusion."

We will often, unfortunately, hear what we want to hear, and Lilly does not promote this case as anything more than "mysterious." But it certainly provided him with incentive and it was not long before he was producing results with other animals which only an arch-skeptic could question.

The contact experiences had progressed with very favorable results, and Lilly had accumulated a huge amount of essential information about sounds, behavior and the nature of dolphins. There had also been a huge heightening of what can only be described as awareness, a mixture of love and respect and admiration which was to dictate his entire approach to dolphins then and now.

At this early stage he was not able, even for himself, to properly interpret these changes of attitude, merely admitting (I suspect to his later cost) to a general and indefinable feeling of "weirdness" at a lecture he gave to medical scientists in 1962.

When one is doing vocalizing experiments with Elvar, one sometimes has the feeling that he is very impatient with our slow and laborious methods. He acts as if he wishes we would hurry up and understand him. He apparently is pushing points we as yet cannot imagine. For example, he sometimes inserts long passages of delphinese alternating with our words as if to translate for us.

It is as if a person or a personality or a being who somehow reaches out towards us, who comes as far as we believe he can come at a particular time, and who seems to be waiting to proceed to the next as yet unknown step.

Equality in its broadest sense had become entrenched in Lilly's mind, and he was beginning to acknowledge superiority. By 1965 he was no longer content to have dolphins contained in test boxes, no matter how carefully these experiments were monitored. It was decided to build a facility—an apartment—in which a human and a dolphin could live as equally as was possible given the differing environmental demands of the two species.

The human chosen was a remarkable young woman called

Margaret Howe, and her roommate was a dolphin called Peter. Margaret and Peter lived together as friends, and something more, for ten weeks. Margaret needed more facilities than Peter, but they were designed to be as integral a part of the shared environment as possible. Her bed hung just a few inches above the water, while her desk, although necessarily out of the water, was attached to the side of the tank and her chair was in the water. For 90 percent of the time she was in the apartment (she had Saturdays off to organize her tape recordings) Margaret and Peter were in direct vocal and physical contact.

Their situation was totally unique. Today in America we have scientists partially sharing daily environments with gorillas and chimpanzees in search of the same kind of communication empathy, but never before or since has a human being presented itself to an animal on a basis of equality, in a situation designed to bring on mutual learning.

In the initial stages of the experiment, little progress was made toward the primary objective—conversation—but a huge amount was learned, the hard way, about how disparate are the worlds of a woman and a dolphin.

Margaret records: "The first few nights in the flooded room were awful. I was uncomfortable and hardly slept . . . I found it was very tiring just to walk across the flooded room."

Peter was having similar difficulties: ". . . some nights he has been quiet but others he just has to yell and splash around."

But as early as the first week, June 15 to 19, 1965, Margaret Howe and Peter made their first breakthrough on the language front, and I would again remind you of the problems such a step represented for the dolphin. "He said, for the tape, one clear word, 'BALL.' This came in the middle of one of his ramblings by himself and it could contain no meaning. But it is good pronunciation."

By the fifth week of the experience (much of the earlier time having been taken up with the extraordinarily complex details of two aliens living together), Margaret was able to report definite progress with language. Comprehensibility is a problem, but Margaret "feels" the sounds were like English—"in the middle of a party it would be considered background conversation."

There is unfortunately no way I can write down any worthwhile representation of the hundreds of English-sounding words that Peter and Margaret exchanged during their eight weeks together. That they were English in content is unquestionable.

But I have sat in Dr. Lilly's sound laboratory where these irreplaceable tapes are now housed and will state categorically that I have heard a dolphin making very commendable attempts, given the problems the animal faces, to speak English. If the same sounds had been made by a human with a speech deficiency, the teacher would have been delighted with the results.

And behind the words Peter calls in his strange high-pitched voice there is a discipline, an awareness of what he is trying to do, which is every bit as important, and perhaps more indicative, than the words themselves.

For example, after sixty-three days of living together, Peter stopped "clicking" or giving any "dolphin" responses. He listened to Margaret's requests and instructions and then he spoke. If he got it wrong or his word was not sufficiently coherent for Margaret she was able to stop him and start again. It was the discipline of a classroom in which the raw student, even if he has not quite mastered the subject, understands the method of teaching and is certainly understanding the lesson and its purpose.

Let us be clear about certain things. No dolphin has yet quoted Macbeth and no dolphin has engaged in any vocal discussion, dialectic or otherwise, with any human. But they have ably demonstrated their ability to learn the human trick of making meaningful noises in air. Their brains, to be considered in detail later, are large enough a computer to handle the complexities of language. I believe that what Lilly and others have proved is ample facility, and to bring the point home a little more graphically and to ensure that no one is left with the feeling that we are somehow trying to justify conclusions on sketchy evidence, I would propose an experiment you may do yourself.

Apart from the various teaching experiments with specific words, Lilly, assisted by Alice White, conducted an extensive series of experiments in which dolphins were asked to repeat strings of "nonsense" syllables—sounds of different type in no particular order of comformity. We will take ten of these syllables for our game: In, At, Oyn, En, Ta, Oh, Oys, Ett, Ray and Mi.

During my visit to his sound laboratory, Lilly played me some recordings of these nonsense syllables being read to a dolphin together with the dolphin's responses. I also heard some of the more famous English word tapes, and naturally my interest, at the time, centered, egoistically, on these. I had heard the skeptical comments that they were garbled and inconclusive, a conclusion which, having actually heard the tapes in person, I don't share.

Only later, when I began to consider what we were actually trying to prove, which surely must be the "intellect" for speech rather than our capacity for inventing speech technology both for ourselves and dolphins, did the significance of the nonsense tapes strike home.

I was sitting on a transatlantic jet from America to my home by the River Thames in London, desperately fighting the boredom of such trips, when I came across a printed list of the nonsense syllables. I read the list and then tried to repeat them! I turned to a colleague in the next seat, explained the background and read him the list. He tried to repeat them.

So here is the game. Sit down with your family or a friend (children, I have discovered, are often better at this than adults) and read them the list of nonsense syllables above, at a normal reading speed.

Do not be too depressed if they cannot manage to remember more than five of the sequence. That is a fair human average.

Lilly's dolphins, as I know from listening to the tapes, copied with a fair degree of accuracy all ten disparate sounds immediately after a human utterance of them. The dolphins copied the sounds with fair accuracy, but more important they not only got all ten but delivered them back at virtually the same rate, with the same pauses, at the speed at which they had been delivered —and did so at first exposure, without practice!

Just what do we think we are testing? All human words are nonsense to dolphins. For all they know, because we have no way of telling them, the gaps between the words, or the nonsense syllables, are as important to the game as the words themselves. So what do they do? They hand back everything, more accurately than any human can match. Or, more simply, a game from which we seek only word sounds is treated by the dolphin as a comprehensive, multifaceted mathematical game. By comparison, speaking just the words—if we can somehow explain to dolphins that that is all we want—would obviously be a much easier exercise than the complex absolute response they give now.

All the communication experiments, in particular those involving speech, now point unquestionably to the need for a huge jump in human understanding of dolphins. A talking dolphin could admittedly tell us a great deal, and the desire for communication is understandable, particularly if one considers purely pragmatic human needs. It would be immensely useful to employ the world's dolphins to supply a much-needed map of the ocean and the ocean bottom. It would almost certainly solve the energy shortage, at least temporarily, by revealing the existence of oil-bearing strata. A communicating network of dolphins would instantly revolutionize marine weather reporting and be of untold benefit to shipping. Dolphins herd fish naturally, work with tools of their own when the need arises and can be taught to handle some of ours with the bare minimum of training. If we could therefore inform them of our food needs and train them in fish-farming technology, the problem that most threatens the human race would be solved in a very short period of time. Yes, the rewards are obvious.

For me they are too obvious. And they are designed only to benefit humans.

The dolphin can provide man, by example, with a better and longer-lasting solution to these problems, but that will involve a quantum jump in our concept of values—of those things that are of real importance to man.

I see no point whatsoever turning the dolphin into the slave of man simply so that more men can expand into more territory (it would have to be the dolphin's territory eventually) and there use up more food, more oil, more natural resources. It achieves nothing but an extension of time for the prevailing disastrous values of the human race, and I think we can do better than that.

When I speak of a quantum jump, I mean a leap beyond the obvious. It is not even a trip into the unknown anymore, because we know enough about dolphins to have confidence in their ability to tell us more of many things than can be conveyed by a human language.

I was able to see a classic demonstration of this "out of the unknown phenomenon" when we recreated at Harderwijk a very famous "speech" experiment conducted in America in the middle '60s by Dr. J. Bastian. Using lights and levers, two dolphins were asked to talk to each other underwater. Dolphin A was shown a flashing light which corresponded with a lever that had to be pushed successfully by dolphin B. You will not be surprised to hear by now that the dolphins passed the necessary information quite successfully.

The experiment at Harderwijk was slightly different from Bastian's, and by employing better recording equipment the Dutch scientists hoped to establish which sounds the dolphin was using to pass the information. Even though the test was made much tougher (one of the Harderwijk dolphins was blindfolded with rubber suction cups to ensure that it could only operate via the sound messages it was receiving from the other dolphin), 250 runs produced a success rate of 95 percent.

The Dutch team jubilantly turned to their tapes of the sounds passed, convinced that the squiggles on the oscilloscope would show what could be termed the first words of "delphinese"—"push the right lever" or "push the left lever." Some weeks later they reeled back in a state of confusion, forced to face the fact that the dolphins either had some method of communicating that we had never suspected, or that something had gone seriously wrong with the recording equipment.

None of the instruction sounds matched up! "Push right" in Test 1 was a particular squiggle—but "push right" (the same message) in Test 20, and so on, was completely different.

There was endless speculation as to what was happening. Could the dolphins have some compressed message system which allowed the same thing to be said in a different way? Were they bored after the first few runs and engaging in high-speed chats—"You remember that stupid button I asked you to press a few shots ago; well, for pity's sake press it again so we can get off to supper," all in a rattle of clicks. Were they telepathic, their sounds simply idle chatter?

One way or another the experiment was a classic example of the successful failures dolphins inflict on man with monotonous regularity.

Finally, Dr. Peter Purves was called to Harderwijk as an independent observer, and he quite quickly spotted what the dolphins were up to. They aligned themselves up slightly differently before pulsing out the "push right" or "push left" signal. This gave the beam of their signal a different quality, a quality the receiving dolphin was able to recognize and use.

But what did it give the scientists? A failure experiment? More evidence that dolphins could not really speak to each other—or evidence that we have only scratched the surface of their communication potential? This is what I mean when I speak of the need for a leap beyond the obvious.

Dr. van Heel, who is an enlightened scientist, pointed out that the method being used by the dolphins was an extremely successful, efficient method of passing the message. Or to look at it another way, when you have as many systems of communication as the dolphin is now known to possess, language as we know it may well rate as an inefficient, labored, time-wasting method of passing information.

We can hardly expect the dolphin to revert to Dinosaur by choice even if they do have some motivation for wanting to communicate. The very least we will need to do is attain some knowledge and proficiency at the level they have reached if we are to have communication which is anything more than primitive.

I would go further and suggest that attempts to have the dolphins communicate with us via a human language may well create confusions so immense as to block the search for effective communication. For example, Japanese friends of mine have told me that because of the complex nature of the Japanese written language, schoolchildren have to do something like three times as much work to reach the same college standard as students studying and writing in English. Some Japanese, concerned that their country keep up and remain competitive, have started to advocate teaching in English. Why should Japanese schoolchildren suffer increased labor, the frustration that goes with pointless work, in the interests of nationalism?

Why should dolphins? Were it not for the fact that dolphins appear to have an interest in learning, an extraordinary quality of tolerance, and old Plutarch's gift of friendship without reward, I think they would have quit long ago. Most human beings would.

And how would we have judged the dolphin then? I suspect that because we were unable to invent an effective—and, yes, intelligent—method of communication we would have let the dolphin slip back into the sea along with all the fishes.

Fortunately some humans have gone beyond this point with dolphins now, and John Lilly leads this enlightened elite. We will give him the last word in just a moment, but I think Margaret Howe, who after all is the only human being on earth to actually get down and do what all the rest theorize about, deserves a moment here. Wet, bedraggled, slightly chewed, often depressed and working always close to the point of complete exhaustion, this amazing young woman wrote in her concluding notes:

"Let us be open to the possibility of learning and practicing what we learn from the examples set by the peaceful, gentle and (not to be overlooked in a time when ulcers and nail biting are part of our every-day life) happy dolphin!!"

Lilly, I know, endorses this wholeheartedly, even if his fears of man are a little more advanced. As he put it in a lecture delivered in Chicago as long ago as 1962:

One can protect one's self by maintaining one's ignorance by belittling disturbing experiences, or one can newly recapture sensitivity and be open-minded (even painfully so), and *discover* new facts.

Discovery in my experience requires disillusionment first, as well as later. One must be shaken in one's basic beliefs before the discovery can penetrate one's mind sufficiently above threshold to be detected. A certain willingness to face censure, to be a maverick, to question one's beliefs, to revise them, are obviously necessary.

But what is not obvious is how to prepare one's mind to receive the transmissions from the far side of the protective transparent wall separating each of us from the dark gulf of the unknown.

Maybe we must realize that we are still babies in the universe, taking steps never before taken. Sometimes we reach out from our aloneness for someone else who may or may not exist.

But at least we reach out, and it is gratifying to see our dolphins reach also, however primitively. They reach towards those of us who are willing to reach towards them. It may be that some day not too far distant we both can draw to an end the "long loneliness" as Loren Eiseley called it.

As Lilly has illustrated here, communications research—the search for the speaking dolphin—has point only if we regard it as the first step in communication. Speech has very little to do with the problem.

Two decades of research do little more than show us that talking is somehow irrelevant. But that in itself is something, because it has at least pointed the way for us and dolphins if we have the perception to see the way. In the meantime, both men and dolphins have a variety of methods of communication, and we can manage quite well until the technology necessary for us to speak a common "language" is forthcoming, as it surely will be.

Hold hard to your seats, because I propose to suggest that the most effective tool of communication we have at our disposal at the moment is that hoary, much-maligned, much-abused human faculty with which the dolphin is also abundantly endowed—love.

SEVEN

"What All Great Philosophers Seek . . ."

HAVING spent the last chapter being somewhat contemptuous of our attempts to get dolphins to speak our language, let me make it very, very clear that I am not against *communication*.

In fact, the prospect of real communication with dolphins appeals to me as the most productive, exciting and stimulating exercise the human race could engage in at the present time.

We should recognize that the dolphin is a being from another world and that a real interchange of information would be every bit as enlightening as an exchange with a being from outer space. Possibly more so, because whereas an extragalactic would almost certainly be the evolutionary product of a world very alien to man, dolphins are alternative forms here on our planet, where we will always be most at home.

It is also becoming increasingly evident, especially among the young, that the age-old values of the human race have become considerably tarnished and, in many cases, unacceptable; or more simply, we are in need of alternatives.

I have already listed the obvious advantages man would gain from dolphins—they could unlock the door to a forbidden two-thirds of the total area of the earth, the area covered by sea. There are some physical advantages for dolphins as well. We would be obliged to stop slaughtering them in huge numbers and, more important, end the very serious extinction threat posed by our use of the sea as a huge industrial sewer.

But far and away the most exciting aspect of a real exchange between dolphins and man is concerned with essential knowledge, basic values and life-style concepts; and these are not as esoteric as they may appear at first glance.

It is very hard to conceive of a species embodying so many contradictory elements as does the human race. At one level we are still in the caves. A gas stove cooking the Sunday roast is a minute step up from a cave fire barbecueing a leg of antelope. We still congregate in aggressive tribes, we still relegate our women to a secondary role, we still arm ourselves to the teeth and we still fight wars for essentially the same reasons as we fought them a million years ago.

On the other hand, we value education and abstract thought, induce our young to aspire to greater knowledge, and have made huge advances in our arts and our sciences. We have universities expanding our concepts of philosophy and ethics and we have legal systems based on essentially correct morality. Half of our split personality has a lot to offer.

Dolphins are inquisitive, avid learners with mighty brains, and the interest they have shown in us is a clear indication they would like to learn more—I believe, all there is to learn. But they seem to have overcome the dangerously primal drives that still lurk in man and live by principles of nonaggression, expansive friendship and sensory empathy which are intriguingly similar to the principles of the alternative life-styles now being tried by some human groups. Or to boil this down to something more direct: the main extinction threat to man is man himself; there is a very good chance we will wipe ourselves out, either slowly by denuding the planet of the stuff of life or quickly via the nuclear button and the germ-warfare plant. Dolphins do not face this crisis. They have evolved a system of living together which is apparently free of territorial aggression and the territorial imperative. They are safe from themselves, and if we could understand the complex fabric—the emotional social structure—which makes this possible, and learn from it, we would become safe from ourselves.

There can be no greater incentive for communication between the two species than this, but it is also fairly obvious that the kind of communication we need goes far beyond speech. It will need to be a bond of understanding based on deep emotions, with love, in the broadest sense of the world, and respect as the basic platform.

In 1966 a number of enlightened scientists began to consider this difficult concept when they staged a debate entitled "Communication with Extraterrestrial Intelligence." The discussion ranged across a broad field, including technical problems and the simple factor of probability, but among the speakers was John Lilly. He confined himself to dolphins as an ideal extraterrestrial case study and spoke openly about love and emotion as an element in communication. It was, he said, a vital element.

Lilly explained that a number of people had been lost from the dolphin research program, and he advanced this rather strange cause:

"Sometimes we think that these people who are lost are projecting their own hostilities outward onto the animals. The people who survive either realize that this mechanism is operating and conquer it, or else their nature is such they do not have hostilities to project."

Although the terms are vague, Lilly, from practical experience of a human/dolphin program, here succinctly identifies the importance of the emotional fabric in the communications exercise. He is saying that "projection" is not, like television, a single source of images. It is a fine weave of the emotions playing like a variable electric current between two sources, each as unsure, as confused, as ignorant, as the other. The only way to overcome these essential, but obviously critical, problems is trust, or, as we make progress, that expanded version of trust, love.

I believe that the general basis for this kind of trust and love exists between dolphins and man, and it can be recognized in the indefinable "lure" that the dolphin has always had for man—and vice-versa. It is also time I stopped hiding behind the word "indefinable" when referring to the lure. Let us make an attempt to define it, and for the pragmatists who may have been wincing at my suggestion that love is a valid format of communication I will at least attempt to follow a chain of logic and stay within a few scientific terms of reference.

Behavior

We will start with a simple statement of the obvious—that the dolphins do appeal to people—and break down why. A great number of clinical scientists whose training preempts instinct judgments (and almost anything with an emotional tinge) have now been lured by dolphins via just this process.

They have in fact made a fairly comprehensive study of this "luring factor," and bracketing it is an area of study called "behavior." I propose to go a step further and suggest that behavior patterns should not be a one-sided study. All right, we will never understand dolphins unless we are totally cognizant of the patterns of their behavior, but it cannot surely stop there. We must also consider our reactions to their behavior and face up to the outcome.

For that, in a sense, *is* communication, and communication, be you scientist or layman, is the Grail.

My first hint of this interrelationship of fact and fancy came when certain scientists who had taught dolphins exercises designed to prove certain unknowns—sonar, hydrodynamic ability, depth facility, memory, hearing and so on—stood back far enough from the actual point of their research to wonder at the ease with which their subjects had learned the mechanics of the tests.

Or, more simply, they asked the question, Who teaches who?

Let us start with ourselves, the audience at a dolphinarium show. We sit and we watch. We even, as I have been intrigued to note, applaud. What do we applaud? At first a gymnastic ability—much as we applaud and admire the athletes of the high wire and the trapeze. Then, at subliminal levels, an awareness of intelligence, a growing sense of equality. This is not a fish, not if it jumps on command, can judge distance and angle, will turn as a group, pick up the towing rope of a boat and carrying one of our young around the pool. We, the dolphinarium audience, are lured.

And there is something more which I frankly do not understand—if you like, do not have the qualifications to understand. Dolphinarium shows are "prime viewing" for the very young and the very old. At either end of Shakespeare's seven ages of man we expose our kind to the lure of dolphins. There is something here which is important, for the human animal is at his most compassionate—at his most emotional—when dealing with the very young and the very old. Perhaps—and again may I admit that I am describing an emotion of my own, not proper understanding—we realize that here, in the context of these sublime performances, there is something our species needs to see in its formative time and may understand when peace, and possibly wisdom, is cloaking the mind in the ease of old age.

Or to put what I have expressed as a hazy emotion into a more gutsy form for all of us to chew on, try Herman Melville's description:

"These are the lads that always lie before the winds. . . . if you yourself can withstand three cheers at beholding these vivacious fish, then heaven help ye. The spirit of godly gamesomeness is not in ye!"

But certainly more important to the point I am trying to make, this fascination is not lost on the scientist. The research facility at Harderwijk, as I have indicated earlier, is financed by a dolphinarium circus. This particular circus is, in my experience, unique in that it has deliberately incorporated into the show the findings of the research pools that are concealed behind walls and that the public do not visit.

Harderwijk dolphins, for example, find and recover sets of plastic objects which have been designed, according to their specific gravity in water, to float at different levels in the show pool. One set stays on the surface, the second hangs at half the depth of the pool, the third sinks to the bottom. The audience is advised that dolphins have complex sonar abilities and then shown how it works—with a fast-swimming animal flashing around the pool neatly collecting the three widely dispersed sets of target objects in its beak.

The same dolphins leap through hoops from either side of the pool, demonstrating the dolphin's extraordinary ability not just to agree to jump but to so coordinate their movements as to leave the water in an agreed sequence that will cause two animals to fly through the hoops at the same time.

A trainer hanging over the pool from a high ladder with a herring in his mouth is not demonstrating his own courage or the dolphin's greed but the dolphin's ability to leave the water, adjust the lens of his eye for accurate visibility in air and compute the power/time equation that is necessary to reach the target.

Small wonder that at the end of a show involving perhaps twenty such tricks, the audience leaves with a general admiration of the dolphin species while the scientist ruminates as to the real mechanics underlying such a performance. And ruminates in a way which is an insidious contradiction of his discipline; as confusing and perhaps as simply "alien" as the dolphin is to the entire species of man.

I remember in particular an exchange which graphically illustrated this dilema, when that most committed clinical scientist, Dr. Purves, was asked a speculative question after admitting that dolphin sonar was an ability we had not yet completely tested. Was it possible, if a dolphin could read the contents of a swimmer's stomach, that they might not be able to read the thoughts and emotions of another dolphin's mind or even man's mind? That they might in fact be capable of telepathy?

"That," Dr. Purves replied, and I have no wish to suggest that he is, or was being, any more evasive than any other scientist of his reputation, "is a metaphysical type of question and I really cannot answer it."

"But," the question was put, "can you rule it out?"

To his great credit, Purves replied, "Perhaps not."

In the same arena, Dr. van Heel, a more extroverted man but no less a clinical zoologist, is more forthcoming. I suspect this stems from the fact that the Harderwijk facility is Dr. van

Heel's pride and joy (there is no other way to describe the odd mixture of clinical objectivity and pure animal interest that he gives to the place) and that he spends so much time there in an office that is actually under the main dolphin pool.

We were talking about Harderwijk's emphasis on passing on "scientific" findings in the form of tricks in the show. He had been presented with my now rather overrepeated quote of Plutarch about "disinterested friendship" and this had brought forth the traditional lecture on anthropomorphism—which I feel you should hear if only because it is, in a sense, the protective barrier behind which the scientific establishment attempts to entrench its objectivity.

Of Plutarch, Dr. van Heel said: "That is anthropomorphic thinking. It is seeing something from the outside, from our side, and applying it to the animal. As to 'disinterested friendship,' it is honestly something we have not the slightest idea of. We do not know. As a result there are two streams in the study of animal behavior—one that may be called animal psychology, which thinks there may be something like feeling, etc.; the other the ethologist view, which says we know nothing about feelings and that animal behavior must be studied from an objective point of view. Animals must be treated as objects; they must be viewed at a certain moment and all subjective feelings forgotten."

But contact with dolphins makes this separation of viewpoints almost impossible. I would go further and suggest that science has made a somewhat simplistic mistake (if understandable in terms of the kind of thinking required if one is to combine the two approaches) in trying to separate the two. I have not the qualifications to suggest the model of a psychologist/ethologist animal behaviorist (the term alone conveys the complexities) but it seems to be increasingly obvious that such a hybrid is necessary.

For example, having delivered his lecture on the dangers of anthropomorphism, van Heel went on to make a number of observations which are somewhat anthropomorphic. He had been staring across his office at a dolphin playing behind the armored-glass window; the animal was obviously trying to attract our attention, or certainly was interested in our activities.

Abruptly he spoke: "We know there is something. They have certain feelings, but whether you can go so far as to say they have philosophical minds I do not know. I cannot say that yet. But it looks . . ." He paused and glanced again at the dolphin. "You are tempted all the time to think so."

And then he shifted abruptly to another subject, which I believe (in that it came to his mind at that point) to be related to his doubts about what the dolphin may be truly capable of. It concerned an incident involving a trainer who was trying to get a dolphin through a hoop with a distinct lack of success. Finally van Heel was called on for help, and on going to the pool he noticed that the hoop was being held in an awkward position in relation to the dolphin and he suggested that the trainer move his hand. The dolphin immediately soared through the plastic circle, and van Heel went back to his office to ruminate, as he has ever since, on just who was training who. Had the dolphin, as he put it, "heaved a huge sigh of relief" when the trainer had the sense to set the ring right? Or more specifically, had the dolphin, by refusing to try the awkward leap, finally trained the trainer to hold the ring properly?

The "trainer or the trained" dilemma so fascinated a filmmaker friend of mine, Richard Wade, that he spent some time at Harderwijk making a documentary called *Who's Training Who*, of which the following is his own summary:

Taking into account that as a filmmaker my interest has always been in people rather than things, it's hardly surprising that faced with dolphins, my immediate attitude was to study them as "people."

My film was called *Who's Training Who*, which should give a reasonable clue as to what it was mostly about. There was a certain amount of scientific material involved, but in the main, I was concerned more with their personality and the way in which they use their intelligence rather than to study how scientists have proved—or failed to prove—how much intelligence they have.

I worked closely with a trainer in Munster called Martin Huygen who, without any scientific background whatever, stated that dolphins have at least as much intelligence as men and probably a great deal more. To me, his experience over several years was quite enough to convince me without any further scientific proof. Even so, I was amazed to discover the reality of their sense of humor. To me, the classic joke is not the man who slips on a banana skin, but the person who carefully steps over the banana skin and disappears down an open manhole. I am sure that dolphins would love that joke. It is exactly how their sense of humor works. I became friends with one dolphin who delighted in spitting about a pint of water straight in my face when I wasn't expecting it. Not particularly subtle, perhaps, but the lengths he went to to disguise the moment when the water was about to land firmly in my eye were brilliant. He would bob up and down affectionately until the exact moment when he had convinced me that today I was not going to be soaked. At that moment, in a flash, aimed to within half an inch, came the water—splat! He would then leap up and down, quite obviously delighted with his achievement.

Of course, scientifically, it is easy to say that this does not prove anything at all. True. It is also equally difficult to prove that scientists who make such suggestions have no sense of humor themselves. Humor, thank God, is still impossible to define in terms that a computer can understand.

When I was about sixteen, I used to sail a 14-foot dinghy in Table Bay off Cape Town. There was a dolphin there who used to come and play around the bow of my boat. He also had what seems to me the same sort of humor. He would bob up regularly on one side of the boat chattering loudly. He would go on doing this, until he had me leaning out regularly to talk back to him. Having got me moving satisfactorily like a pendulum, he would come up again at exactly the same interval of time, only on the other side of the boat. He fooled me every time.

To my satisfaction, dolphins know when they are being filmed. One of the dolphins at Munster has a trick in the regular public performance which involves getting up on his tail and "walking" backwards for half the length of the pool—some 15 or 20 meters. When I set up the camera to film this trick between the shows, he obliged by not only going backwards for the entire length of the pool but coming all the way back again, "walking" forwards. Something he'd never done before. Three weeks later, I returned to get some bigger close-ups of various tricks, including this. We asked him to perform and again he went all the way back and all the way forwards. He had never done it while we were away and, as far as I know, he's never done it since.

When the film was finished, it seemed to me that there was no reason why I shouldn't follow my normal practice and show the film first to the people featured in it. I like to give my subjects the chance to say what they like of what I have done to them. At Harderwijk in Holland, there is a large breeding pool with a glass front designed so that members of the public can stand and watch these most beautiful creatures swimming lazily around inside the pool. We set up a translucent screen on the glass of this pool, and with a human audience on one side we showed the film (in mirror image) to about five dolphins inside. Two of them were less than two years old and had been born in that very pool. While the film was running I spent my entire time watching the dolphins. I was almost the only person there who had seen the film before. Their interest was extraordinary. In the sequences of explanation—dolphin shape, hydrodynamics, sonar etc.—they took obvious interest. Admittedly, they may only have been excited by the play of colored lights. When it came to the jumping sequences, however, several of them started leaping out of the water and at least twice I could see that the jumps they were doing were, in miniature, the same jumps being shown on the screen. It may have been coincidence but I doubt it and I feel sure that as it is the only occasion that I know of when dolphins have been shown a film, it is worth trying an experiment to see if it is possible to make educational films for dolphins. Making educational programs for humans is a thankless task at the best of times, and I suspect that dolphins might be a great deal more appreciative.

I only regret that so far nobody has discovered how dolphins could be persuaded to make films about us. It really would be a breakthrough if the dolphins could explain why *we* behave the way we do.

I have never met a diver whose entire attitude to the sea has not somehow been changed by contact with wild dolphins and this includes scuba enthusiasts who can hardly bring themselves to leave the ocean. I suspect the enhancing effect of dolphin contact has a lot to do with dealienating the sea for human beings. Essentially it is a strange and hostile place for us, fraught with many dangers and inhabited by species that are very alien to mammals. In the main, these creatures are not dangerous to man and the risk, even from creatures like sharks, is exaggerated—but there is no question that the creatures of the sea are very different from us and the submarine world is not a place where we can feel at home.

Contact with dolphins changes everything. Firstly they are obviously intelligent and their awareness and interest in a human diver instantly sets them apart from the instinctive reactions of fish. Their shared need to surface for air extends the bond and there is something more, something to do with their incredible command of movement in the sea. I have always felt, when swimming with dolphins, that they would assist in some way if ever I were to get into difficulties. This has never actually happened to me, but there are a great number of well-documented accounts of dolphins assisting swimmers or people who have been shipwrecked.

It would also seem to be the case that the more intimate and extended the contact between a human and a dolphin the more intense the "change" brought about in the human, and this change is not simply enhanced respect. It involves a complex amalgam of emotions.

The best documented account of a contact between a diver and a wild dolphin concerns an Englishman, Dr. Horace Dobbs and a dolphin called Donald who makes free use of the inshore waters of the British Isles. Dr. Dobbs has written of his experiences in a moving book *Follow a Wild Dolphin* (Souvenir Press). This story is particularly interesting because the murky—and invariably icy—waters round these islands is an unlikely place for so intimate a relationship to have occurred even though dolphins of Donald's species—the bottlenose, *Tursiops truncatus*, are quite common around Britain. There are a number of records of these animals stranding themselves in the heart of London—having injudiciously swum up the River Thames.

Dr. Dobbs met Donald via another diver, Maura Mitchell, after Donald had struck up an intimate friendship with Ms. Mitchell in the sheltered waters of Port St. Mary, Isle of Man.

By the time Dr. Hobbs got to meet Donald he was already the regular friend of a number of local divers; in fact, he was making something of a nuisance of himself with the Manx fishermen.

Dr. Dobb's arrival on the scene was fortuitous not only because he began to make Donald famous and thus protected, but also because Horace Dobbs had all the qualifications necessary to compile a detailed record of this friendly wild dolphin. He is a pioneer underwater photographer with impressive diving qualifications—the rare First Class certificate of the British Sub Aqua Club.

He is also a clinical scientist not overly given to emotional judgments. In spite of all this, Dr. Dobbs was so affected by the four years he maintained a contact with Donald in different harbors around Britain, it literally changed his entire life and, most significantly for me, gave him a concept of freedom that he now regards as his most treasured possession.

After a series of brief meetings with Donald he decided not to continue his career as a successful radioisotopes chemist and veterinarian. Instead he would "freelance" as a diver—and study Donald.

"I was going to run for freedom," he explained. "I felt as excited and as eager as a young man stepping out to conquer the world, and confident that I could do it."

As indeed he could. Over the next four years, Donald changed homes five times, moving from the Isle of Man to Martin's Haven in Wales, and then to three different locations in Cornwall.

Everywhere he went Dr. Dobbs followed him, photographed him, studied reactions and behavior and entrenched what Dobbs himself describes as an "extraordinary friendship." On all but one of these occasions, Dobbs found Donald through reports from local divers, but when he made his first move, Donald, and no one can ever say how, found Dr. Dobbs.

Dobbs set out in August 1975 to run an underwater photographic course at Dale Fort on the furthermost southwest tip of Wales, but as is so often the case with diving in British waters, the weather intervened and the dive was moved to Martin's Haven, some 200 miles from the Isle of Man where he had last seen Donald. It is worth mentioning that Donald was never tagged in any way nor was any radio pack or locating equipment ever attached to him. He was always, in every sense, a wild, free dolphin.

Dr. Dobbs was sitting in a diving inflatable talking about photography when he heard what he describes as a familiar loud puff alongside the boat:

"What I saw next was almost unbelievable, for out of the misty waters came the cheeky grey face of Donald. From his movements I knew there was no mistaking him but who would believe me? We were over 200 miles from his old haunts."

As time went by Dr. Dobbs was able to call Donald with a rattle and eventually with a small trumpet that transmitted a better sound underwater. Their contact was physical and involved a lot of games, but Dr. Dobbs was also able to begin what almost amounted to an educational program with Donald. The dolphin was intensely curious about everything, particularly mechanical and sound-emitting devices and liked to touch them with his snout. Sometimes this inquisitiveness got him into serious trouble; he was badly cut by the prow of a boat he investigated too closely, and on another occasion stayed too long under a boat and was stranded by the tide. A band of human friends doused him with water and then trundled him back to the sea, somewhat unceremoniously, in the bucket of a mechanical digger.

Throughout the long years of their relationship Donald displayed the dolphin's legendary lack of aggression—with one bizarre exception. Dr. Dobbs once showed him a mirror and he smashed it on the spot. But as Dr. Dobbs commented, it must have been a fairly unnerving experience seeing another dolphin looking you in the eye, especially as Donald's other senses, like sonar, would have been telling him nothing was really there.

And there were more than enough rewards to balance this one agitated moment. Quite early in the relationship, Donald picked up Dr. Dobbs' thirteen-year-old son and gave him a ride round the harbor on his back; later when Dobbs got to know the animal better, he was able to ride Donald himself.

"Faster and faster we went. Soon he was going full speed, and I was still clinging to his dorsal fin, the sea swirling up in a white foam round my face mask and shoulders. On and on we went in a huge loop."

Dr. Hobbs sums up his relationship with Donald as follows. It is a poetic description of the effect that a dolphin can have upon a human.

"Scientists will be sceptical, and rightly so, about this joy that people say they feel when in Donald's presence until some more tangible evidence can be produced. But until someone invents an instrument to quantify it and measure it . . . we shall have to be content with the evidence of our own subjective experience."

Dr. van Heel, Richard Wade, and Dr. Dobbs share a reaction to a similar experience in these reports, but the degree to which they are prepared to accept the evidence, or more correctly, to interpret the evidence, shows something of the impasse we have come to with dolphin research. In a society conditioned to definable qualifications, the scientist is our ambassador to the unknown. But in this area of communication via emotions, instincts, and feelings, traditional disciplines make it difficult for scientists to express such views.

Richard Wade is not concerned at being labeled an emotionally subjective thinker, an anthropomorphist. As his report shows, he believes he has to open his mind in this way to make effective contact with dolphins. Dr. van Heel, whose opinions would carry more weight in science, is very concerned and must hedge his impressions. Many scientists have less courage and say nothing at all about instinctive concepts, although, in my experience, they all have them.

It would seem to me that we are thus artificially limiting our understanding of dolphins and placing substantial impediments to the prospect of real communication. More important, I do not believe that Dr. van Heel's impressions or Richard Wade's convictions can be rejected as scientifically invalid any longer. They crop up too often to be inconsequential and are, in my opinion, the observations of a new group of ethologist/psychologists; new because for the first time we are in contact with an animal species, the dolphin, which is infinitely more complex than any we have studied before.

Man's great attribute, and probably the dolphin's as well, is that he is the most sophisticated and complex computer in the known universe. Clever machines are, and will be, increasingly capable of "ethology"—plain, observational assessments. But the extraordinary mammal brain/computer is capable of something much finer, infinitely more complex: the computation of amalgams of emotions, abstract values and clinical observation.

I have, however, promised to follow a logical progression and stay within the area of scientific reference, so we should consider the ethologist's purely behavioral findings. They are the basic building bricks of communication, and every one of these findings has strengthened another aspect of communication—respect.

Sexual Behavior

Since the time of Dr. Freud, sexual behavior has been accepted as the primary factor in communication; the quality, sensitivity and complexity of sex is a valid pointer to the level of development of a species. There is a huge and significant difference between the procreation of worms and the complex love play and mating of human beings.

When, in the '60s, ethologists began to observe the sexual behavior of dolphins, the immediate reaction was bewilderment verging on shock. We were witnessing a display of erotic activity and sexual empathy that rendered human sexual behavior as simplistic as the pragmatic copulation of chickens.

Dolphins engaged in love play with almost everything in sight—with brothers, mothers, fathers, daughters, cousins and aunts. There is even a well-documented "ethologist" note of a dolphin masturbating with a herring.

Dolphins were heterosexual, homosexual and asexual as the joyous mood demanded. And this behavior was so normal—so obviously contained within a framework of love and absolute enjoyment—as to make these conservative human terms irrelevant. They enjoyed a sexual Utopia that exceeded human fantasy.

It was, of course, another and significant pointer toward an advanced status; a very advanced status if we are right in our theories about the difference between worms and human beings.

Family Behavior

It took a long time for scientists to be able to study family behavior, because dolphins, seemingly content to live in captivity, were not so content to breed there. It was many years before a baby dolphin was conceived and born and survived long enough in a dolphinarium for the experts to study it.

Now we know more about looking after the babies, there have been many such births, and we also know that the dolphin, no matter what you may think of its sexual proclivity, is a caring, loving and rather strict mother.

Harderwijk has a good record of live births, and while I do not wish to particularly favor this one center, it seems better that I write of instances of which I have personal experience, so again I will quote Dr. van Heel. This description is "ethologist" in content, but look hard and I think you will see something else leaching through:

> In the beginning when the baby is born, the mother stays very close to it and teaches it how to react to her call. Then after a few hours the baby learns to stay close and swims almost as if glued to the mother, perhaps a foot away. It is beautiful to watch, the constant maintaining of position by mother and baby is perfect. Every movement the baby makes the mother echoes, or perhaps it is the other way around.

This deep maternal affection of cetaceans has been known for years and used by the whaling industry. They would quite deliberately harpoon a baby whale knowing that the mother would always come to her young. There is the case of the pilot whale at Marineland of the Pacific, Los Angeles, California, which apparently regarded a striped dolphin who shared the tank as its baby, or at very least, in a maternally protective role.

When this particular dolphin died, the pilot whale took the corpse between its pectoral fins and stayed with it, rising only to breathe. Eventually a diver went in and harpooned the dead dolphin, attempting to retrieve the corpse via the cord attached to the harpoon—but the whale would have none of it! It rose to the surface and caught the dolphin in its mouth in such a paroxysm of anxiety it smashed a heavy steel gate and cut itself badly. The whale snapped the cord and bent the harpoon before returning to the bottom of the tank with its dead friend/baby. This behavior went on for five hours, with the whale constantly retrieving the dead dolphin, until finally divers managed to sneak the corpse away. When called upon to perform in a show, the whale refused.

How such an emotional pattern of behavior could be coolly and calmly observed defeats me. But indeed it was, and the ethologist report of the incident by Melba and David Caldwell and David Brown was published as "Intergeneric Behavior by a Captive Pacific Pilot Whale."

Domestic caring by dolphins is not confined to blood relatives. Dolphins are loosely labeled "herd animals," a term used, I conclude, because their group behavior patterns have been little studied and a school of dolphins appears closer to a herd of antelope than any other example in the natural kingdom.

I have observed herds of land animals in several African game parks, and all they would seem to have in common with groups of dolphins is that they stay in groups. Certainly a pregnant wildebeest about to give birth does not get the kind of caring attention an expectant dolphin mother gets.

There are well-documented accounts of dolphins taking turns supporting a sick animal on the surface when it would otherwise sink and drown. Some researchers have concluded that this is the reason dolphins have been known to push human swimmers to the surface—our inept movements in water being taken by the dolphin as evidence of illness!

At Harderwijk I was personal witness to an extraordinary sequence of events involving a sick dolphin mother. A lot of people who run dolphinariums believe an impending birth is communicated to the other animals—in fact, they use this phenomenon of "nervousness" and a general falling off of interest in the business of the daily circus as an indication that a pregnant mother is coming to term. There are virtually no other signals available to humans standing by to give antenatal care.

At Harderwijk, a pregnant dolphin miscarried. She was living in her own pool near the main large show pool, and when the miscarriage began, the "atmosphere" altered dramatically. All the dolphins immediately lost interest in their other activities. One animal was sent through to join the ailing mother and swam with her for several hours until the dead fetus had completely miscarried. Several others gathered in what was obviously an anxious group behind the bars separating the main pool from the "maternity ward."

An attempt was made to run a show, an audience having gathered while all this was going on. It was a complete farce. Show animals who normally performed like clockwork patently had their minds on something else. In fact for the whole of that day, long after the mother had recovered and had been moved to a pool well away from the show pool for medical attention, the dolphins behaved as though someone had dropped a hand grenade in the water—they were shocked.

Perhaps more intriguing, this behavior was not confined to the dolphins. Harderwijk has recently acquired a young *Orcinus orca*, a killer whale, which is the largest species of dolphin. In the wild, killer whales sometimes eat dolphins, but during the period of the Harderwijk crisis this animal, although it was a baby and had been in captivity for a matter of months, exhibited the same kind of anxiety and concern as the mature dolphins. Because of its size it was decided to isolate the nervous killer whale in another side pool where it could still see the dolphins in the main pool. Throughout this period of confinement it made distressed squeaks and whistles and spent most of the time with its huge head jammed up against the wooden grill that led into the main pool.

Dolphin mothers combine affection with strict discipline. Van Heel has seen a disobedient youngster tossed squealing into the air enough times for it to learn a lesson and not wander away from its mother's side. Once when a ball was thrown into the pool to amuse a boisterous youngster, the mother spent some time inspecting the ball and throwing it about herself before she would let her child anywhere near it.

Play Behavior

But having come to this subject of play, we should pause and take a very careful look at it, for it is in the area of play that dolphins excel above all other species, including man, and play is not the simple mindless activity it at first seems. It is in fact the only behavioral guide to intelligence we have ever managed to identify.

Some few years back, a young writer, Richard Neville, whom I was later to get to know quite well, wrote a book called *Play Power* which was to become, briefly, the Bible of what might be termed the Flower Power movement in Europe. *Play Power* received a brief burst of publicity when it was published, even though its thesis was anathema to established society. It suggested that man, in the building of his groups and systems, had destroyed one of the most vital aspects of the human psyche, the ability to play. The work ethic, Neville suggested, was no more important (and in his terms less) than the play ethic, if happiness was the goal.

At the time, I was (and I suppose still am) driven by the work ethic, but I can recall being strangely disturbed by Neville's essential point—that play is part of the life force and that Western societies' obsession with work status might be wrong rang some hidden primitive bell in my mind.

That same bell rang again, this time stridently, when I saw my first dolphins on a regular basis off the Azores and began to realize that a great deal of their life was spent in play.

The tradition of dolphins following boats has been on record as long as there have been records. Cretan and Minoan friezes include exquisitely drawn dolphins convoying the ships. Dolphins use the various waves created by boats for a kind of underwater roller-coaster ride, surfing these pressure planes for pure fun. Pragmatists have suggested that they use them for an easy ride, but if you have ever been in a boat with dolphins alongside this explanation is nonsense. It makes no difference where you are going—the dolphins come along for the trip.

I experienced this most vividly during my three-month sojourn in the Azores, where we could literally not avoid the local dolphins. As soon as our diving boat cleared Angra harbor they were there, a cloud of shifting shadows all around the hull. They very much preferred our big power boat with its large wave-making inboard-outboards to the divers' inflatables, which moved through the water with much less disturbance. It seemed as if our arrival had been expected—as indeed it may have been!

At that time I was not aware of the comprehensive nature of dolphin communication systems, but we did notice that dolphins would come into Angra harbor of a morning around about the time we began the lengthy procedures involved in getting a team of twenty divers and their equipment shipped. It happened so regularly as to exceed coincidence and eventually became something of a team joke—with one of our people calling out to the dolphins, "Hang on, we'll be out in a minute."

Our dolphin companions were also completely unafraid of any human activity. We often had to maneuver erratically in those rough, rock-strewn waters and were initially worried about hitting the dolphins as they swam everywhere—under and to the side, front and rear of the boat. Our fears were groundless; they could shift position like quicksilver, and if anything, high-powered turns seemed to improve their ride.

Our expedition photographer, Pat Baker, armed with a motorized camera and full diving gear, once threw himself backward over the stern of the boat when we were traveling at 20 knots with a huge school of dolphins riding the stern wave. Firing his camera like a machine gun as he bounced and submerged, Pat got the action pictures he was after. He also reported that none of the dolphins deviated from their fun ride when his ungainly, black-suited shape crashed down among them, and not one of them came near to colliding with him.

Some may argue that this is all constructive play—that dolphins play better if you give them something to play with; but that surely is hairsplitting. In the open ocean, dolphins gambol, leap, spin, turn on their tails and ride the bow waves of our boats out of a pure sense of fun and enjoyment. It is a huge part of their lure.

But is it something more than that?

I had advanced some of the *Play Power* arguments to an eminent zoologist and suggested that if Richard Neville was right, possibly dolphin play was yet another indication that the species was ahead of man in its development; that a life of play was part of our concept of Utopia, and the dolphin had already built it into his life-style and had accorded it an important place.

"I can see what you're getting at," he replied. "But I think you may be stretching the neoteny factor a bit far."

I was forced to ask what the neoteny factor was, and the reply was as follows.

Zoologists judge the intelligence of animals according to their levels of neoteny. Neoteny is the ability of an animal to play as an adult.

It is not a difficult scale to see if you start applying it to a few species. Calves and lambs gambol but stop dead in their tracks when they become sheep and cows. Chickens have brains so small they don't even play as chicks.

But start applying the neoteny factor to larger-brained animals and you begin to see how the scale works. Puppies play, but so do adult dogs, if less than when they were puppies. The same is true of cats. Most monkeys play quite a lot as adults—chimpanzees most of all. Man, for all his Protestant work ethic, will play a game of golf or tennis if he can find the time off from work. And dolphins play all the time!

So far as I know, no one has yet made a calculation of the amount of time dolphins spend playing, or how much time man spends in games, but from my own professional studies of humans and dolphins at work and play—and I have been writing and making documentary films about nothing else for fifteen years—I have absolutely no doubt which of the two species stands highest on the neoteny scale.

No doubt the skeptics will try to reject this as well, even though neoteny is a scale conceived by the scientific establishment; perhaps by suggesting that dolphins do not have a mature sense of enjoyment but purely childish natures. I don't think you can have it both ways—dolphins are obviously highly intelligent, as our every contact with them has proved. A high neoteny level fits this interpretation rather than childishness.

In fact, the deeper one digs into the pure ethological findings, the more evidence comes to light in support of an advanced intelligence.

Mechanical Behavior—the Use of Tools

One of the measures man uses to judge high intelligence in animals is their ability or lack of it to use tools. This has always seemed to me to be a desperately human-oriented test, for only man has had to depend on his hands and tool usage to an important degree. Admittedly our use of tools has made us what we are. From the first animal bone used as a club, through the first flint used as a knife, to, say, the modern laser tools, man's achievements are the sum of the things he has built with tools. Even the arts are tool-dependent—painting on the brush or the palette knife, music on instruments—and we employ a further set of tools to propogate the arts—microphones, cameras, television. This book was typed and later printed. We might argue that intellectual thought, concepts of philosophy, etc. do not require tools, but their dissemination does.

Only in the latter half of this century has our obsession with tools been questioned, and then only obliquely. The "return to nature" cult is generally dismissed as extremist. In fact it is the extreme end of a wedge that has been driven deeply into the societies of the prime tool users, the developed West. Its more popular face is the ecology lobby, the antipollution argument and the growing rejection of cities as a fit place for human habitation. What we see here, particularly with cities, is machines or, if you like, tools that are breaking down coupled with a general realization that the tool-dependent society is overusing its tools in the exploitation of limited raw materials.

Animal life has never separated itself from nature, but man has left it far behind and we are at last beginning to realize that we have gone too fast.

For many years I have held the view that the dolphin Utopia was the result of this animal's sublime affinity with nature, but you will find this a hard argument to propose to the zoologist or the anthropologist. Almost to the man they regard animal dependence on what can be termed simply body tools—hoofs, horns, teeth and claws—as evidence of slow evolution.

For many years, then, I sought a tool-using dolphin, hopeful that this phenomenon would cause a cry of respect as significant, and as status-building, as Jane Goodall's revelation that chimpanzees in the wild were not scratchers and grabbers but genuine, if simple, tool users.

I did not conduct this research for myself—how anyone could question the ability for tool-using intelligence in dolphins after watching them adapt to human devices in a dolphinarium pool has always defeated me. But the answer you get is that this tool-using has been taught, in the same way as chimps at their tea party can be taught to pour from a pot. It is not an innate ability, not the great bridge that took man from anthropoid ape to human status.

In 1977 I was able to visit a number of the large American sea circuses and heard a number of possible examples of dolphin tool usage, all too vague for my purpose. Then, at the Seaquarium in Miami, someone casually remarked, "What about that business with the moray eel at Marineland?"

I felt like Jason after all his problems with the Golden Fleece. Admittedly it was not a current observation, but it had been well documented by Brown and Norris as a definite incident at Marineland of the Pacific. I was also very intrigued to note that this positive use of a tool was a by-product of a dolphin game.

The two Marineland dolphins were attempting to provoke a reaction from a moray eel. Moray eels don't normally come out to play, preferring to keep most of their snakelike bodies well anchored in a rock crevice while they defend the entrance with impressive flashings of their formidable teeth. The dolphins had sense enough to know that these teeth are not just for show.

So while one of the pair kept the moray eel diverted the other swam off in search of a tool. It spotted a scorpion fish, which has sharp dorsal spines, grabbed the fish carefully so that these spines stuck out and returned to the foray with the moray. Making speedy jabs at the eel with the scorpion-fish spines, this tool-using dolphin finally poked the eel from its shelter and then proceeded to use the eel itself as a tool for a game of toss and catch.

In summary it may be said that the ethologist's behavioral studies of dolphins have proved the animal to be of high intelligence, social, responsible, gregarious, a tool user with a neoteny factor that is arguably higher than man's. There are two mountain peaks in the animal universe, a Japanese scientist aptly and poetically put it, and on one sits man while on the other sits the dolphin.

But as I suggested earlier, the clinical approach of the ethologists is an inadequate method of studying dolphins if the purpose of our studies is to establish the basis of real communication between dolphins and man. It promotes respect, which is one step along the road, but it cannot take us the rest of the way into broad emotional contact.

Fortunately some researchers, people who I believe fit my description of ambassadors to this great unknown—the ethologist/psychologists—have made a start down this very difficult road.

Emotional Behavior

Dr. Sterling Bunnell is a psychiatrist and an ecologist, but most important, if his work is any guide, he is a very original thinker.

He has come up with a theory which is not only a revolutionary theory of communication but makes irrelevant every concept that has so far been advanced about how and why dolphins behave as they do.

In an article which I read in a book called *Mind in the Waters*, Bunnell quickly ran through a superb description of cetacean evolution and the cetacean brain and then folded their sound and echolocating abilities into the mix. From this batch of clinical ingredients he came to the following conclusion:

> Extreme playfulness and humor are conspicuous in dolphins. . . . Despite its low status in puritanical value systems, play is a hallmark of intelligence and is indispensable for creativity and flexibility. Its marked development in cetaceans makes it likely that they will frolic with their minds as much as with their bodies.

If you find this concept as hard to grasp as did I when I first read it, it is worth breaking down the equation by which Bunnell arrived at it; and it is certainly worth it if you consider what such a possibility does to all the equations other scientists are laboriously pursuing by the search-and-prove process.

Bunnell arrived at mental frolicking by taking an original look at the echolocating ability of dolphins and the fact that they can transmit that information. As a start, he noted that the dolphin's language seemed to consist of complex sounds, arriving in units (my Ping-Pong balls are primitive but will do). Great chunks of information were arriving in parcels. He then turned to the echolocating ability and realized, accurately, that they were getting very detailed pictures. I have described them as three-dimensional. They are certainly extra-dimensional in human terms. He then adds these two known facts together, and asks the question, Could the dolphin be sending these extra-dimensional pictures in parcels to others? Bunnell uses the example of Chinese characters, but I think there is a better media example.

A television set translates a chain of electrical impulses into a picture by spreading those impulses as lines of light dots across a screen. What I think Bunnell is getting at (and the known facts about dolphin sonar and interspecies pulsing support him at least technically) is that dolphins are sending to other dolphins complete pictures direct to the brain. And I mean complete—so complete as to make my television example very primitive. These would be three-dimensional images, emotively described, not just a flat image on a screen. Each dolphin would—and here one sees how beautifully Bunnell has chosen his word—frolic in the mind (and for that matter with the mind) of the animal with which it was in contact.

There is nothing in human language which can equate with this. What it does support, and with a vengeance, is the need for minds like Bunnell's to be applied to dolphin research, for if he is wrong, he is only wrong, but if he is right, or only half right, then we will not arrive at communication with dolphins via the step-by-proven-step method, any more than Baird would have discovered the principles of television by studying semaphore.

Another reason for choosing to place Bunnell's theory here is that it is very difficult for the layman (and I include this lay writer in that group) to break away from his own conditioning and accept that he may need to dabble with the unknown in order to accept some of the findings of enlightened dolphin researchers. It is not just the scientist who is subject to limiting disciplines; they are, as I have said, our elected representatives, and they do no more than express, if in an exaggerated form, a general human conservatism.

Such conservatism, if applied excessively to the more advanced experiences in the human/dolphin program, will bar us from sharing these experiences because they limit us to a low level of acceptance. I am appealing for an open mind in our own interests and in the interests of these researchers—in particular for the work of Miss Margaret Howe, who has already been introduced. You will understand what I mean more clearly if I remind you that it was Miss Howe who went to live with a dolphin for two and a half months. We have so far dealt only with her work as a sound recordist. It is time we faced the fact that this was *the* "behavioral" study and, quickly, while the mental door is still open, that Margaret and Peter Dolphin made love.

Love, you will recall, is what this chapter is about, and Margaret Howe's "life" with Peter Dolphin locks "behavior," "love" and "communication" together inexorably.

I have already described the apartment Margaret and Peter shared for two and a half months, and the complete experience is described in detail in Lilly's *The Mind of the Dolphin.* In the fifth week of their relationship Margaret grows concerned that this is being hindered by a developing sexual attraction. She can have physical contact with him for only so long before he becomes sexually aroused.

Thank heaven for the existence of a free mind at this surely traumatic turning point. Margaret's reaction is positive—"I found that by taking his penis in my hand and letting him jam himself against me he would reach some sort of orgasm."

And my inclusion of this incident is in no way vicarious, for as a product of her totally serious committal to the "living together" experiment, Margaret establishes a relationship with Peter which exceeds any before, and so far as I know, since. Toward the end of the ten weeks, Margaret records her reaction to spectators watching from the side of their shared pool; her irritation with Peter, who reverts to silly games, and her own boredom and annoyance at the antics and gestures of the human spectators. "Peter is not in a cage," she writes angrily, "and will not be played with, teased, observed, stared at or anything else by 'outside' people. Peter has outgrown you."

And as John Lilly notes alongside this account, "And so has Margaret."

So what were the conclusions of Margaret Howe, who is almost the only human to involve herself in dolphin behavior rather than observe it artificially either through windows or the refracting surface of water from the side of the pool? I found her most telling reflection to be that concerning superiority. Margaret had read Pierre Boulle's *Planet of the Apes* (the best satire in print on the subject of species superiority) and had used it symbolically to consider the relation of man to dolphins:

"We must face the thought of the two equal intelligences on equal footing on this planet. This may well already exist, with the only missing link being communication."

But she is not using communication in a simplistic sense. Let us say that one day we can speak to dolphins. What questions will we ask? If you look at the main dolphin reasearch programs I suspect the questions would come out like this: "How can we eat the food reserves of the sea? How can we find oil-bearing strata? Would you guard our harbors against Russian submarines (or U.S. submarines if you are Russian), or drive fish into our nets?" Human-oriented questions, all of them. Personally I suspect that communication may be much farther away than even optimists like John Lilly have allowed themselves to think, not because of problems with technology but simply because we are not beings like dolphins. Would you be prepared to allow a dolphin to frolic in your mind, or to get to the point, make love with you?

Which brings me to the most important point of all regarding dolphin behavior. Is that in fact what we are studying—is that even what the ethologist is studying? From the time I first heard the word "ethology" (and from the moment I first had to defend what was termed "anthropomorphic thinking") I have had a sneaking suspicion that it was not just the words that had become confused, but the very attitudes behind them.

Let us look again at the two ways of studying animal behavior, starting with a simple question: Why do we study animals at all? I don't think there can be any doubt that when Professor Brunowski looks at animals he is in fact examining how superior is man. But even when you move on to someone less biased, like Ardrey, we are still in the area of animals vs. man, admittedly in the nicest possible way. I do know one man in Kent who is devoted to fleas, but even he has made a calculation that if we had flea spring ligaments we could clear the Empire State Building.

And consider the public sense of wonder at scientific findings. We prick up our ears if they relate to us—Jane Goodall captured everyone's attention when her savannah chimpanzees were spotted killing game for food (like man); Konrad Lorenz presented his thesis that the basic patterns of human aggressions are to be found in most animal species and in particular in fishes; C. R. Carpenter's howling monkeys defended territories as man defends his; Jean Jacques Petter's Madagascar lemurs enacted certain ways of man, although they are fifty-million-year throwbacks; Lauterbach's bowerbirds built "tents" and offered inducements to passing females. Even the lowly planarian worm was shown by Best and Rubinstein to be capable of boredom, teachability and a lot of human compulsions.

Somewhere, someone I am sure is seated before a microscope or up to his waist in tropical mud, concerned only with worm worries, fish freedom or bird building; but in the main, and it is a significant main if we consider why we study animals, we are primarily interested in relating everything to ourselves.

And I am no exception. This book is an undisguised platform for dolphins directed at man. It has been cast in that mold deliberately, as propaganda for dolphins, because I believe that our studies of animals—and these include dolphins—are in the main overt propaganda boosters for man. You may even like to review the facts and findings that have particularly interested you in this book. Were they not in fact those dolphin capabilities which were somehow an extension, a comparison, of some human capability?

We are still standing on either side of a species divide while our objective, communication—the product of a deeply emotional mutual respect—waits in the middle. Margaret Howe again with her shining light of understanding:

"We must face the thought of the two equal intelligences on equal footing on this planet. This may well already exist, with the only missing link being communication."

Is there any example we can find to nudge man off his high horse, one to which we give unquestioning love and respect even though it can be seen as a primitive animal? How about human babies? For a moment be objective enough about a human infant to see it as it really is, a little object that cannot walk, talk or feed itself, giving no indication that it will turn into an adept, garrulous, perambulating adult.

A psychologist, Andrew Locke, used this perspective to lead him to an understanding of the attitude humans must adopt if we are ever to break through the communication impasse with dolphins.

Dr. Locke, you may recall from an earlier chapter, had gone to the Morecambe dolphinarium in England, after hearing reports from the trainers Stuart and Shirley Gallagher that the dolphins were "taking over the show." Locke made the enlightened decision to study this problem from a different viewpoint. He set himself to study the two humans and their behavior toward the dissident dolphins of Morecambe.

I know of only one other case in the study of communication where this perspective has been used, dealing with, of all animals, a horse called Clever Hans. At the turn of the century a German mathematics teacher concluded, it appears quite innocently, that he had discovered a horse that could read and figure. By nodding and shaking his head, Hans the horse did sums and became the wonder of his time. Unfortunately, an examining board took a very close look not at the horse but at his questioner, which revealed that Hans was being cued by inadvertent gestures made by the teacher.

Andrew Locke considered the gestures being made by Stuart and Shirley Gallagher to their Morecambe dolphins, but went one considerable step further. He also contemplated the obvious attitude of love and affection the Gallaghers had for their charges and began to think about this in the context of other studies he had been doing about mothers and their babies.

He explained to me that he began his study with the question: Were the Morecambe dolphins behaving like human babies under the loving and maternal care of the Gallaghers? Babies don't talk at birth and are unable to convey complicated concepts, but their mothers think they can—know they will—and their mothers communicate with them *as if* they can. The child grows up to be able to do what the mother thinks it can do—because the mother has that essential belief.

It may help to look at this backward. Would a child learn to talk and express itself if its mother never communicated with it? No, no more than the mother would bother to try (or more accurately treat her offspring as if it were already a conceptualizing, talking entity) if she did not think it was one.

To relate this to our problem with dolphins, we block out the possibility of communication if we do not start with love and respect and a belief in their ability to communicate. Stuart and Shirley's dolphins were learning *because* they were being "anthropomorphic"—believing in their animals' abilities, and more important, "communicating" with respect from the start.

Locke quoted the example of work in America with chimpanzees. Prior to this work no one had thought that chimpanzees could talk. But treat chimpanzees as potential talkers and find the right tools—in this case deaf-and-dumb signing—and chimps talk. Even more interesting is the work being done in California by Penny Patterson with a young gorilla called Coco. I went to see Penny and Coco during a visit to San Francisco in 1977 and discovered a situation which would have driven an ethologist into a state of frenzy. Coco was being treated like a five-year-old child, taught table manners, discipline, social (human) behavior and language. Admittedly, Penny, who is a slight blonde, had been reduced to a pale and rather nervous shadow by her 500-pound child (the similarity to King Kong and Eve was extraordinary), but the fact of the matter was that Coco had learned some three hundred words, was expressing them via signing in complex sentences, and was conveying emotion and even signaling her intentions—the nicest example being a morning when Penny told Coco she'd had a bad night and Coco confessing that she was not happy that morning and had cried.

Chimpanzees we have always treated with some intellectual respect (expressed somewhat sadly by dressing them in human clothes and staging chimpanzee tea parties at the zoos), but the dopey, lumbering, chest-thumping brute gorilla?

Andrew Locke has no doubt that this is the right way to communication, and I share his view. The ethological method of so-called objective observation is of no use all the time the ethologist is human, believing what we see of behavior is all there is to see. Penny is making a complex scientific study of her charge, but it is not ethological in form, and her results are infinitely more rewarding as a result. Here again we see the evolving ethologist/psychologist and further evidence that my suggested "hybrid" is the valid new form of clinical researcher.

"As a scientist," Locke confessed, "you tend to think this is not the right thing to do. But the more time I spend with these animals—dolphins—the more difficult it is not to entertain the idea that they have something more than one initially expects."

And he added: "Intelligence seems at the moment as though it might be phenomenal. I don't really know how much that is the interesting question, because you find an IBM computer has a phenomenal intelligence. Certainly dolphin intelligence is great—but there is something extra with it."

He also made an extremely interesting observation of relationships between the Morecambe dolphins and the audience, the word "relationship" being synonymous with "communication" in this context: "One is aware of an immediate relationship between the dolphins and children."

Could it be that the much-vaunted wisdom of "babes and sucklings," expressed, we believe, accidentally, is in fact an innate ability to communicate, later blunted by the development of set beliefs or an excessive insistence on mental discipline? Or even something more simple. I have said earlier that man has a high neoteny factor—that he plays into adulthood as a demonstration of the highest intelligence. I remember when I wrote this that it might be an egotistical human assumption, because if one thinks about it hard, eccentrics, as we call the mentally playful, and nonconformists in general are the human exception rather than the rule. More, our social rules do no more than tolerate nonconformity, and this in spite of the fact that according to science it is a manifestation of advanced intelligence.

When we first met, Andrew Locke was in the middle of his research program, and suffering what to him was a new, but as known from others, disturbing, feeling of confusion. "In honesty the more I studied them the more confused I became rather than enlightened." And he confessed that as a psychologist his experiences at Morecambe had made him stop and take stock of what he had been doing up until then. Another evolving psychologist/ethologist, perhaps?

Human Behavior—the Interrelationship

The previous section has, I hope, established that an important factor in dolphin behavior, especially communication, is human behavior. The communications block is almost certainly coming from entrenched attitudes and a lack of respect and faith on the human side.

Fortunately this situation is changing and more and more scientists are acknowledging somewhat "unscientific" doubts, questions they cannot answer, and a general if unprovable fabric of respect. It might be said we are being dragged reluctantly toward real communication.

Picking through my notes of conversations with Dr. van Heel I came across the following, which are random in nature but consistent in form and very typical of the things clinical scientists say at the tail ends of lectures or in what to them would be unguarded moments.

"It is the emotion . . . the wonder . . . that you are dealing with an animal which is on a high level. . . .

"There is something . . . something more moving than we can comprehend. . . .

"One is aware that everything is on the margin—on a frontier —and there are aspects we dare not present for fear others will say, Humbug!"

Out of these vague and apparently equivocal phrases it is quite simple to pick out echoes of love and respect—the basic platform for the kind of real emotional communication we are seeking with dolphins.

But in the phrase "there are aspects we dare not present for fear others will say, Humbug" we also have the human block to communication neatly identified.

All right, humans are a stubborn breed conditioned by a hard evolutionary road to believe that survival means keeping our guards up. But we have made that an outmoded, unnecessary concept. Man's enemies have long since fallen back from the gate, and what we need now is contact with intelligent friends if our species is not to atrophy at its present level of development.

All we have to do at this stage to communicate with dolphins is to sit back and enjoy them with open-minded friendship. A mutual "interest for no reward." Or if you like, and this time I offer no defense for the phrase, mutual love and respect.

EIGHT

The Largest Brain on Earth

IF the facts and figures so far revealed have augmented any race fears rather than calmed them, you might do well to skip this chapter, because the dolphin brain, if judged through the fractured lens of interspecies fear, is intimidating. Those still with me, those concerned to judge this brain objectively, will still need some courage.

The situation is this:

If we are careful, we of the human race; if we do not engage in practices which will render ourselves and our world extinct; if we go on developing our brains at approximately the same rate as over the past few million years; it is vaguely possible we will have brains comparable to dolphins in about five million years' time.

I base that calculation on the following: Man's prehominid ancestors of some five million years ago had brains which weighed, at best, 500 grams. Modern man, the product of an evolutionary climb that placed mental ability under continuous and powerful growth incentives, has a brain weighing about 1,450 grams on average. Let us say we have trebled the weight of our brains in five million years.

One of the uses to which modern man has put his enlarged brain is the elimination of many of the threats that caused him to develop it, so the indication could be that growth in the future may slow down. For the sake of this equation, however, we will accept an ongoing mental growth rate for man and speculate that five million years in the future we will have brains three times their present size.

The fact, the fact that must be faced, is that many of the cetaceans have brains four to six times the size of man's already. We would reach parity sometime in the mindless future. The brain race, if we are foolish enough to see it as a race, is well and truly lost, because, of course, for us to even catch up with the cetaceans, their brain development would have to cease.

We are not the largest-brained animals on the face of this planet, never have been and never will be!

As is true of most statistics, these straight comparisons are of no importance other than in the context of human competitiveness, and this book is not concerned with such idiocy. In fact, it is significantly intriguing that at about this point in many of my chapters I have been forced to state that such and such an ability "does not matter." This is particularly true of the huge, and certainly awesome, cetacean thinking mass. To recapitulate, it is not hydrodynamics that matters but how the body is used; it is not speech that matters but communication; it is not brain size that matters but the mind and in particular the nature and the potential of the beast that is formed by the mind.

If we accept that definition then the brain of the dolphin is of great importance because it is not just a very large brain but a somewhat more complex one than ours.

But most important, it is large enough, complex enough, subtle enough, to service the kind of expanded contact there could and should be between man and dolphins.

We have three brains, dolphins have four. No, I am not back to a species comparison; their extra lobe we compensate for elsewhere. And all the evidence would indicate that dolphin and human brains developed by the same method unique in mammal anatomy. Or to put it more accurately, our brain organs and those of the dolphins were forced to make their improvements very differently from other parts of our body.

Such was the pressure on the brain brought about by the other evolutionary changes going on in mammal bodies that the brain was never able to switch off—it was, after all, making all the decisions. Something had to be in charge while the human body was standing up, expanding its skull, developing those tricky fingers, blunting unwanted toes, shedding hair and so on. And if this was true of man it was doubly true of dolphins, who were discarding unwanted appendages en masse, fusing their heads into their bodies and adding totally new mechanisms—a fluked tail and a stabilizing dorsal fin.

You couldn't throw away a redundant brain in the same way as you were abandoning a leg or body hair. The best you could do, as has happened with vital human facilities like urban hospitals, was to build on a new wing, and another and another.

There can surely be no more awesome thought in the natural universe than that we still have the oldest wing of the hospital inside our heads—the same brain that our most remote ancestors had to manage with thirty million years ago. It is surely as close as we will ever get to proof of our own immortality.

When that original brain, the reptile brain, known as the limbic node, could not handle the computations of the evolving mammal body, a new wing was added by folding a second brain around the limbic node. This, called the cortex, was the think tank for the mammals during their great leap forward. Having taken care of survival and the facilities for conquest in the case of man, and adaptation to the full dimension of the sea in the case of dolphins, a third brain was added, the neocortex. That is the rough shape of the human and dolphin hospital of the mind today—a trinity of intellect embodying everything we have ever been.

Just to keep the record straight, the dolphin's fourth brain, called the paralimbic, can only be called an extra in that it is a separate brain lobe concerned with specific sensory and motor functions. In man it is thought we have these brain functions spread as a less well-defined structure around the limbic (termed by human neuroscientists the supralimbic). But I do not propose at this late stage to return to the comparison controversy, for it is not with the reptile brain (and in particular human pride over what, at best, must be a super-reptile addition) that we are concerned.

Dolphin and man enter our arena when they begin to look like dolphins and men. This, in the case of man, occurred, being generous, about two million years ago.

In my souvenir junk box I have a small (and probably illegal) scrap of gray rock from the desert floor of a bleak canyon in northern Tanzania, Olduvai Gorge. I am not normally a kleptomaniac, but who could resist a sample of the floor once trodden by our oldest ancestors—the "apeman" Zinjanthropus, as its discoverers, Mary and Louis Leakey, were to call it.

This upstanding apeman was a wall builder, pebble-tool maker and skilled killer. As Herbert Wendt describes them: "The descendants of prehominids created civilization, waged wars, developed ethical doctrines, denied their past and to this day are fond of emphasizing their exceptional place in the kingdom of living organisms."

Zinjanthropus had a brain weighing approximately 750 grams.

As we know, something very strange happened to the first "line" of the cetaceans. The most ancient whale ancestors, or so the fossil record indicates, seem to have vanished into the hungry vacuum of evolutionary time. But even ignoring these lost relics, identifiable cetaceans were populating the seas of the world in Eocene times, some thirty million years ago. All the indications are that these earliest of modern cetaceans had brains weighing in excess of 1,000 grams.

This figure of a 1,000 grams of brain weight is very important because it is at about this size of brain that we begin to see in our own species the emergence of what we would generally describe as intelligence. It will emerge later that "intelligence" is a very loose and dangerous term—no better, say, than the word "universe" as a description of the void in which we all hang.

But with a little more definition, "intelligence" will do for now. In a normal child (a child whose brain is growing at the average rate), intelligence slowly expands as the brain grows from about 400 grams at a few weeks to 900 after a few months; blossoming into embryonic "adult" forms like speech at around eighteen months. By this time the child's brain has reached at least 1,000 grams in weight.

Humans whose brains do not reach the 1,000-gram threshold do not develop normal, or, as I would personally rather have it, broad, intelligence. These "idiots," "imbeciles" and "low-grade morons" suffer from an insufficient mass of cerebral cortex; they have stopped at an age of evolution, in brain terms, that is the world of Cro-Magnon and Neanderthal man, 150,000 years ago.

Normal children go on to become teenagers with brains of some 1,300 grams and then adults of some 1,500 grams.

Dolphins start with bigger brains and end up as adults whose brains are bigger still.

In a table comparing the brain weights of bottle-nosed dolphins prepared by John Lilly, it was seen that the brains of these animals developed at approximately the same rate as humans' brains during their formative years but with the dolphin slowly creeping ahead as it reached maturity until, at the end of the chart, the adult dolphin brain was some 300 grams larger than that of the average 6-foot human male. Lest anyone thinks I am "fixing" my figures in favor of the known intelligence of this particular dolphin species, it should be noted that larger dolphins, like the orca, have brains weighing as much as 6,000 grams!

To give these figures some perspective it is also worth noting the brain sizes of other animals: rats, 1.6 grams; rabbits, 9.3 grams; cats, 31 grams; dogs, 65 grams; monkeys, 88.5 grams; and chimpanzee, 350 grams.

On land man stands clear of his nearest identifiable mental rival by a factor of five. In the sea the dolphin and the other cetaceans stand clear beyond comparison; for example the huge tiger shark, the dolphin's main enemy, has a total brain mass of little more than 100 grams.

In the light of these statistics it is difficult to understand the human superiority complex. It appears even more illogical if one examines not just the size of the dolphin brain but the makeup of that brain, the way in which large areas of it have been developed, and for what functions.

Fortunately we know quite a lot about this subject, because scientists have been interested in the dolphin's large brain for a very long time. Before the turn of the century, Cunningham and Hatschek made detailed examinations of the spinal cord and other aspects of the central nervous system, and "differences" (in particular the strongly developed tr. gracilis and tr. cuneatus —the routes of skin and muscle sensitivity) were noted. As long ago as 1932, Langworthy theorized that dolphins had especially well-developed mechanisms for transmitting sensory impressions to the brain. He found that in the thoracic section of the spinal cord the crescents thought to be associated with locomotion were much more strongly developed than had ever been found in land mammals.

Other scientists began to count the numbers of fibers in the most important cranio-cerebral nerves, and this again confirmed the quality and complexity of the dolphin brain, the stato-acusticus nerve alone revealing a huge count of 112,500 fibers.

But in spite of the keen interest, the actual "status" of the dolphin brain continued to be relegated to the secondary, and if you read the descriptions of the early researchers there seems almost to be a conspiracy of denigration.

Bolk and Langworthy, the two most prestigious early neuroscientists, recorded the advanced development of the dolphin cerebellum—but immediately tagged this as a factor of muscle coordination. Langworthy also studied the limbic and the neocortex areas and concluded that they showed "primitive" features of organization.

The best that can be said for the bias of these early researchers (Spitzka had produced a description of the dolphin's auditory analyzer as early as 1886) is that they worked in the shadow of an era that had held any denigration of man's unique status as heresy. Spitzka's studies were made less than thirty years after Darwin's *On the Origin of Species by Natural Selection*, which caused science's most bitter species controversy. Even Langworthy's work at the turn of this century would still have been subject to those censorious echoes from the past.

In any event, as modern research teams moved in on the dolphin brain a great deal of the early work was recognized as being inaccurate and biased in favor of man. This was true particularly of certain dolphin brain functions which had earlier been described as "poorly developed" or even atrophied. In 1965, Olsen and Jansen reviewed Hatschek and Schlesinger's 1902 review of the dolphin's auditory analyzer and found it riddled with inaccuracies. They also looked at the acoustic nuclei and were able to discount an earlier suggestion that the dorsal nucleus in dolphins had completely atrophied.

As John Lilly, whose fascination with dolphins began with a clinical interest in their brains, pointed out: "For many years it was thought that large size did not mean high quality." In 1955 he and seven colleagues from five different American laboratories collected probably the first specimens of dolphin brains that were in good condition, their purpose being to test the truth or otherwise of the theory prevailing at that time that nerve cells in the dolphin brain seemed more sparsely distributed than in the human brain. They established conclusively that the dolphin's brain was "first-class," with cell counts as dense as those in humans.

This cleared the way for other contemporary researchers and caused an enormous increase in interest. Up until then dolphin brain research had been a clinical study of an animal brain of no greater interest than that of chimpanzees and dogs. But now science was confronted with the reality of equality and it made an important shift of emphasis—from "how inferior" to "how similar" and eventually to "how superior."

The main interest was focused on the cortex and the neocortex, for if dolphins and their brains were different from man the differences would lie in these "modern" brain areas rather than in the ancient limbic (sometimes termed the archaeocortex) areas which all mammals have in common.

It might as well be admitted now that we do not know that much about how our, or any other, brains work. One of the world's leading neuroscientists and co-author of *A Dolphin Brain Atlas*, Dr. Peter Morgane, summarizes present knowledge as follows: "It does seem that the quantity and quality of gray matter (especially neocortex) in brains can be taken as a definite index of the relative efficiency of those brains in the regulation of behavior."

A careful, sensible assessment. There are other researchers

who feel they can go considerably further than this, but for the time being we will err in favour of caution and consider quantity and quality of the dolphin brain in line with the Morgane definition.

The cortex, which constitutes half the brain mass in humans (and slightly more than half in dolphins), can be graded according to its complexity of structures. Highly developed brains have lots of layers, are folded and convoluted as though an Italian chef had taken a bowl of thick spaghetti and compressed it into a ball, and have strong pockets of regional specialization. The way the cells of the brain are arranged and the complex patterns they form are also indicative of development.

How do dolphin brains stand up to these requirements? Very well indeed! There are more folds than in the human cortex. There are the same number of layers—six—as in humans. A count of the total number of cells shows that the dolphin has more.

By the end of the '60s, neuroscientists in various parts of the world had arrived at some fairly formidable conclusions about the status of the cetacean brain.

The leading Swiss scientist, Pilleri, working with Kray, had decided that the construction of the cortex was in every way comparable to that of the higher primates. Morgane, famous for low-profile statements, announced that he felt there were sound arguments for considering the cetaceans as "potentially intelligent and highly developed fellow beings." He rather gives the game away with the use of "fellow beings."

John Lilly summarized the findings of his several associates: "As a result of our investigations, it is known that the brain of *Tursiops* (the bottle-nosed dolphin) is a first-class brain, of the same order of complexity as that of the human."

So in forty years scientific research on the cetacean brain had projected the species from animal exhibit to superbeast. Instead of a bias against one was able to detect in certain quarters the emergence of a bias for. Try to conceive of a statement like the following being made even a few years ago by two eminent neurosurgeons (G. Pilleri and G. Brenner) from a platform as prestigious as the Brain Anatomy Institute, University of Berne, Switzerland, and you will realize the kind of status leap the cetaceans have made.

A comparison reveals the amazing fact that some species of dolphins have attained a degree of encephalization [i.e., the "resources" of the brain] equal to that of man. All these animals present not only a high degree of encephalization but also a brain structure equal to that of man. One even wonders if they are really animals.

But aside from the sense of wonder, escalation of status and the general accumulation of information about the cetacean brain, the modern scientist also began to wonder what the dolphin was doing with his brain. Or more simply, they tried to face up to the question that brains of this size and complexity would not have been developed if they were not being used.

Again, Pandora's box! And this the most tricky box of all, because the scientists knew that although it had been the subject of more interest and more research than any other organ, our understanding even of the human brain was essentially basic. The dolphin brain was unlikely to be any easier to understand, and early research confirmed this immediately.

Three of the most eminent American neuroscientists, Jacobs, Yakovlev and Morgane, began a mammoth study of 11,000 microsections of dolphin brains, revealing a cell count every bit as high as in the human brain and a great deal of new information on advanced levels of connection between cells. There were at least as many such connections as in the human brain, and these links are generally regarded as pointers to a brain's potential.

John Lilly also examined these dolphin brain sections and recorded that one of the six layers, that on the outside of the cortex, was substantially thicker than he had ever seen in any human brain. As important, if more intriguing, was the discovery that the "silent areas" in the dolphin brain were also of the same magnitude as in the human brain. Little is known of the actual working of these silent areas—hence the name—but it has been theorized that they are contemporary structures probably concerned with the modern aspects of our psyche. Secondary intelligences, like gorillas and chimpanzees, have much smaller silent areas than man. Examination of the brains of the platanistids—the small dolphin throwbacks of the swamps and rivers—gave credibility to this theory when they showed smaller silent areas than modern dolphins.

It would seem logical to assume that if both the secondary intelligences in the worlds of dolphin and man have smaller silent areas, these have been developed to deal with the more complex and more abstract requirements of intelligence in modern man and modern dolphin.

There was also the complication of the dolphin's alien environment. Most of the functions of the human brain relate to the activity required for a life on land and as such could be identified as a chain of thought/actions. We have become the dominant species on the land by a combination of our analytical and manipulative skills, and we have grown brains to service those skills. We have a morality, an ethic—a general consciousness—that is serviced by a brain that has evolved by these imperatives. And we know a lot about these imperatives.

Dolphins came another way, and their brains came with them. They grew in a womblike universe that is a web of physical and sensory impressions that our brains have never experienced. There is no real anthropology of the sea and its creatures; it is another world.

If there are any divers among you, you may perhaps have shared some of my experiences in the underwater world. Before going to the Azores I took a comprehensive underwater course—it seemed wise if one was about to enter the habitat of, among other things, hammerhead sharks. This course represented a turning point in my consciousness, and lest that seem just another glib use of the word, I will take a moment to try and explain it.

Unquestionably the first and most significant impression underwater is fear. It is consciousness of an alien environment; instant realization of how poorly we are adapted to the sea comes before you even enter the water—when you are required to don some twenty items of special equipment, all of them vital. It is not just a supply of air. There is a weight belt to hold you down, a lifejacket to equalize your buoyancy, a depth gauge and decompression chart and underwater watch to protect you against the bends and nitrogen narcosis, fins to propel you and the various items of special rubber clothing to keep the cold out. Small wonder that when this floundering, overloaded object flops into the water it is immediately grabbed by almost all of our most primitive fears from suffocation to claustrophobia.

But then a magical thing happens! You escape the inexorable tyranny of gravity. Weight ceases to exist and you fly. As your confidence expands you forget that you are in water and breathing from an artificial supply of air.

This is the only real physical definition I have ever found of the word "freedom." In my case its effect upon the mind was dramatic. My thought processes became extended and truncated at the same time. The number of thoughts slid through like speeded-up film, but the process of thinking seemed leisurely and calm.

This is the thinking framework of the dolphin, as much as it is their physical world, and when human scientists set out to discover what they could of how the dolphin brain worked, it was realized that this difference of environment was perhaps the most important single consideration.

The findings quite rapidly began to fit some of the projections. For example, a simple glance at the sea would indicate that the dolphins should have highly developed auditory and tactile senses. It was found that the trigeminal nerve, which supplies tactile sensations to the face, was highly developed.

The layers of the brain are believed in man to be related to intellectual acuity and perception. Sense-projection areas in dolphins, located in the cortex, particularly those receiving auditory and tactile sensations, were found to be more highly developed than in man.

Man is a creature of complex motor functions; our hands alone probably move more often than all the exterior parts of the dolphin put together. Motor activity in dolphins is largely concerned with swimming and vocalization, so it came as no surprise when it was discovered that motor control takes up less room in the dolphin brain than it does in our own. It would also indicate that the dolphin is not only attuned to but has plenty of room in its brain for perception and relational matters, probably more than man.

One of the most interesting of the more recent discoveries came as a by-product of research on humans with damaged brains. In all brains the most modern wing, the neocortex, is generally considered to be associated with abstracts like perception, thoughts and in particular memory. But motivation comes from the oldest wing, the reptile limbic brain, and we need a high ratio of neocortical neurons to limbic neurons. Without this ratio, as in the case of brain-damaged humans, faculties like emotional stability, humor, memory, rational behavior—the basic fabric of a stable creative person—are impaired.

Scientists who had noted the dolphin's ability to memorize complex tests and games, their sense of humor, and their obsession with play investigated the limbic/neocortical neuron ratio and found it to be far higher than any found in even the most extroverted, happy, healthy, intelligent and creative humans.

All of which took the status equation one step further. Bunnell actually dared state it. "As regards our brains and our capacities as individual, conscious beings, we may actually be inferior to some other kinds of large brained animals." And as that statement was contained in an article entitled "The Evolution of Cetacean Intelligence" there can surely be little doubt as to which "large brained animals" he had in mind.

And that is as far as we have got, because on the basis of our existing knowledge that is as far as we can take it. We have reached the barrier of the silent areas both for dolphin and man, and no one has yet been able to effectively explore this silence.

There is only one way around an impasse of this kind, a side road so ill-defined as to be hardly identifiable as a road, and one which the main scientific establishment cannot contemplate—enlightened speculation.

When all that could be proved about the dolphin brain by existing methods had been proved, a small group of researchers (a very small group) sat back and reviewed everything that had been discovered. Some did equations like Bunnell and began to think of concepts like "mind frolicking."

John Lilly decided he needed to go even further back. As he explained, "What I found after twelve years of work with dolphins is that the limits are not in them, the limits are in us."

This realization led Lilly to do his own small equation, one that in retrospect would seem simple and obvious but in fact would involve leaving any identifiable dolphin research program and putting his entire reputation as a clinical scientist at risk. "I had to go away and find out, *who am I?* What is this all about?"

Lilly committed himself to several years of complex cerebral experiments designed to explore the inner workings of a complex human brain—his own. He disappeared into physical and intellectual isolation in search of a mystery, the psyche. In a sense it was an avenue of exploration that established science should have liked, in that it totally disavowed the anthropomorphic approach. Lilly was studying dolphins without even thinking of dolphins! They did not approve of it because Lilly used "strange" tools, drugs and isolation-tank techniques, which are too radical for established science.

But I believe their real disapproval stems from something which looks, at first glance, like a semantic paradox. Lilly told science that if it was wrong to think anthropomorphically about dolphins, it was equally wrong to think anthropomorphically about humans. If we have reached the limit of our knowledge of the human brain, what point in continuing to apply traditional human methods to the search? Lilly disappeared inside his own head in search of himself, hoping that when and if he emerged at the other end he might know enough to be able to make contact, and communicate with another large and poorly understood brain—the dolphin's.

He explained his approach in a lecture to the New York Academy of Medicine:

Scientists, especially in the biological sphere, focus their attention down on a small narrow alley, sometimes but not always to the detriment of the wider view.

Let me quote from Professor Donald Hebb's Hughlings Jackson Memorial Lecture in which he said, "It is clearly implied that scientific investigation proceeds first by the collection of facts and arrives secondly at generalizations from the facts. Speculations and a priori postulates are both ruled out. This is the classical view derived from Bacon and it has been known for some time to be false. No research that breaks new ground will be done in this way. The collection of facts from which to generalize demands the guidance of imaginative speculation."

He added a sentence of his own: "Imaginative speculation must be disciplined by integrative feedback with new facts as they are discovered."

And soon after this, John Lilly, certainly as far as dolphin research in Europe and countries other than America is concerned, disappeared.

It was during this period, with Lilly gone off to explore the "silences," that the comments about him that appeared earlier in this book were made.

Apart from the lecture mentioned above, Lilly had been giving warnings of the "weird" (his word) way his thoughts were moving for some years previous. During his earlier work with the human mind, Lilly had studied the effects of isolation, reading everything available from polar explorers, singlehanded sailors and those in solitary confinement both enforced and experimental.

In the middle '50s he published a series of scientific papers with titles like "Mental Effects of Reduction of Ordinary Levels of Physical Stimuli on Intact, Healthy Persons" and "Experiments in Solitude, in Maximum Achievable Physical Isolation with Water Suspension." Illustrating some of these complex texts are faceless aliens with eye holes like doorknobs and a tube mouth—the latex masks Lilly invented for the subjects of his experiments in water.

These subjects were suspended in warmed, darkened, soundproofed water. Lilly was himself a subject—in fact, it was a rule of the project that anyone who wanted to be an observer also had to be a subject. The results of these early experiments have only marginal relevance to our subject and I have not the space to do them any justice, but they do show a very clear and, in our terms, early dissatisfaction on the part of John Lilly with traditional methods of investigating the brain.

And they show something else which so far as I know Lilly himself may not have noted. Remember we are considering a period some years before he found his way to dolphins, and that he was himself a subject of the water-isolation tests. It surely can be no coincidence, having found that the water "wombs" produced extraordinary movements of the mind, that Lilly was later drawn to minds that live naturally in such wombs—dolphins. Or, when his work with dolphins had revealed that "the limits are not in them, they are in us," he returned to the water-isolation method in search of an understanding of his own mind that would allow him to approach theirs.

He went back to explore an unknown, in itself an immensely courageous step, because his discoveries in the isolation tanks in the '50s could hardly be described as clear:

"When given freedom from external exchanges and transactions, the isolated-constrained ego (or self or personality) has sources of *new information* from within."

"As the levels of stimuli were lowered closer to zero the positive, more blissful, enjoyable states and the positive transference phenomena appeared."

"It is felt that such experiences are not necessarily psychotic, or even mentally aberrant, and after training can be constructive and invigorating."

As has been said, I can do no real justice to these experiments, intriguing though they were, and it would be wrong to report them other than where they fit our brief, which is Lilly's search for an understanding of the human brain.

So we will leave "blissful, enjoyable states" and consider just one phrase from the above, the words "new information," which were obviously very significant to Lilly, since he caused them to be printed in italics in the original report.

This, I believe, is what Lilly went in search of when he had reached an impasse with dolphins. It was not just, as many of his peers have so glibly decided, a freaky fancy with drugs (Lilly was later to use LSD quite extensively under clinical control conditions) and water therapy. He had a special piece of real evidence to investigate, evidence of which he had personal experience—"the isolated-constrained ego has sources of *new information* from within."

And it was not as if he even hid this knowledge from his scientific colleagues. In his lecture in 1962 to the New York Academy of Medicine, Lilly told his audience all about his isolation tank experiments and summarized: "Eventually in those that survive, there is a resolution of internal paradoxes and one abolishes what I call mental time wasters. A greater respect in regard for one's self and for one's fellow man develops as well an increased humility in the face of the unknown within one's own mind and brain."

When I said that Lilly disappeared, I was referring to his presence in established dolphin research circles. In real terms and in line with his promise—"Imaginative speculation must be disciplined by integrative feedback with new facts as they are discovered"—Lilly noted, and published, detailed, complex accounts of his voyages of discovery in the human mind.

To an ever-growing elite of cerebral thinkers these books are visionary masterpieces, and although I know John Lilly would be nervous of the accolade he has become a contemporary guru. "Instead of being a Pied Piper," he said in 1976, "I would prefer to be an effective teacher of those persons who seek to understand what it is that I have to teach."

By 1976 Lilly had pulled out of his power dive into the unknown, even though the book he published that year, called *The Dyadic Cyclone*, has another apparently frenzied title. Here we find a calmer, more assured, more knowing Lilly and—surely significant—the decision to think again about dolphins.

This was in fact not an easy decision for Lilly. In an earlier book he had explained that he had closed the dolphin research establishment in the Virgin Islands "because I did not want to run a concentration camp for my friends the dolphins."

But it is obvious from other references in *The Dyadic Cyclone* that Lilly's new approach to dolphins would draw heavily on his years of personal cerebral research, his new emotional and sensory awareness, and would have very little to do with physical aspects of the animals.

One particular passage vividly illustrates his main area of interest. He had arrived, totally independently, at a conclusion about one possibility of the dolphin mind which mirror-images Bunnell's theory of "mind-frolicking." Dolphins, Lilly wrote,

> do not distinguish between sonaring and communicating, in other words they are quite capable of sending holographic sonic pictures to one another with their communication apparatus. They can use these pictures in symbolic ways similar to the way that we used the printed versions of words spoken out loud.
>
> This implies an immense complexity of acoustic memory and of acoustic portrayal, way beyond anything that we have achieved in simulations, in computers, or in terms of concepts having to do with acoustic effects. Only our most sophisticated and advanced mathematics can even approach an analysis of this kind of system.

Lilly, in my considered opinion, is now capable of making the breakthrough he was searching for when he left dolphins a decade ago. He has dared to define the mind of a human being, and by converting thoughts, emotions, images and visions into word pictures that we may read, he has also drawn aside the veil by which man may at least conceive of the Utopia of dolphins. By revealing some of the subliminal magic of our own psyche he has exposed, by association, the tenuous, inexplicable lure of dolphins.

Of all the chapters in this book this one has been forced to travel some rough roads in terms of medical detail and even rougher ones when we turned from the brain as a machine and considered it as a mind. So something in the nature of a summary is called for.

On our planet, man and the dolphin stand so far ahead of all other animal rivals as to make comparison pointless if the weight and size and complexity of the brain are to be the criteria; and the dolphin is significantly out front.

And yet humankind as a race, and science in the main, regards the cetaceans as an inferior animal. One leading scientist has a published opinion which sets the dolphin somewhere between the dog and the chimpanzee on the scale of intelligence.

Where does such myopia stem from? Racism, perhaps. Human fear. Human arrogance—the kind that kept the theory of the Deluge alive until the age of Darwin in spite of millions of contradicting fossils and the entire science of geology. It has also been bolstered by a piece of scientific nonsense that is implausible even to this nonscientist—the theory that you need a big brain to keep a big body going.

Why? Whales have giant brains—those of sperm whales weigh well over 9,000 grams. The only animals that have come close to equaling the whale in body size were the giant saurians, but even including the freaks with two thinking organs, saurians' brains were tiny. They could, but we cannot, have it both ways. If whales need big brains to service big bodies, then dinosaurs should have had them as well. They had plenty of time to develop them—100 million years.

All right, then, the tenacious scientific argument goes, you need a big brain if you are a whale to cope with the frightful complexities of the sea. Dinosaurs simply rumbled around like ancient tanks, treading all in their path and eating everything in sight.

But this does not stand examination either. The dinosaur did not have that easy a life. Apart from the assault of climatic change, they had dozens of enemies—many their brothers and sisters, admittedly, but all ready and waiting to pull them down at the first opportunity.

If the existence of competition and keeping one step ahead of the predators worked as an evolutionary stimulus on the brain of early man, why not on dinosaurs? Whales had conquered the problems of their sea world fifty million years ago. Apart from man, and he only recently, nothing threatens them. They should not, by what might be termed the "easy life" equation, have needed to develop their brains at all. The fact is they have—sensationally.

So enlightened thinkers like John Lilly look for something else.

The only equation that fits the fact that in spite of a non-competitive environment, in spite of their total command of their sea world, the cetaceans have continued to develop their brains—very, very large brains—is that they must be using them for something else. That something may well be a mental expansion into what I have termed Utopia.

The reason we find this world of creative activity and sensory enjoyment difficult to conceive of is that we are still only approaching its threshold. It is little more than ten years since significant groups of human young began to seriously question traditional goals of career — success, fortune hunting and power politics — and to seek complete alternatives, a "better" life and, if you like, a Utopian dream.

And beware the temptation of labeling these admittedly embryonic experiments as the games of effete drop-outs. In the same time period, our most conservative, pragmatic planners have concluded that we are heading inevitably for a society in which the human work ethic will have to be radically reshaped; that our technology, particularly our machine technology, will produce more leisure, not more work.

Hovering on the threshold of this new estate, we find the prospect daunting. To be "unemployed" involves status guilt, and social scientists quail at the thought of the enormous problems involved in converting a work-oriented society to one engaged in stimulating leisure. It is a terrifying paradox. Having overconditioned ourselves to a work role in the interests of building an advanced technological society, we now find it well-nigh impossible to overcome that conditioning and enjoy what we have built!

To cross this threshold we need all the help we can get, and if the dolphins have already made a form of transition, as the evidence of what they are doing with their advanced brains would seem to indicate, it is an example we cannot afford to ignore.

Or, as Robert Ardrey was quoted as saying at the beginning of this book, if we were in a position to regard our knowledge of man as adequate in our negotiation with human circumstance, we could embrace the world of animals simply to enjoy the intrinsic fascination. If not, the wealth of information concerning animal ways "must be regarded as a windfall in a time of human need."

There is one problem with this particular windfall. We need it, we can use it, and it is one of the few valid pointers to an alternative way of enjoying tomorrow on which we may call. The problem is that like almost everything else on the face of this earth, we are exterminating the dolphins.

NINE

Lament for the Doomed Dolphin

THERE is a very distinct chance that we will never enter the kingdom of the sea on a sharing basis with dolphins. There are several strong pointers in the human mentality and in our practices to indicate that when we do make it into the sea we will have emptied it of intelligence.

Our search is not for equality and sharing, we humans of the late twentieth century. We are still about conquest. Consider the facts and you will see that the likely destiny of the dolphins at the hands of man is extermination.

I will start with the broad mentality of modern man, or more accurately with a consideration of those parts of our mentality which are primal yet still exist in us.

It may seem that by allowing in recent chapters the growing respect of dolphin researchers to go on record, I have undermined my thesis—that there is a broad, pervasive and very unpleasant trait of denigration of the cetaceans prevailing in the human race. This is not so, because these respectful scientists are a mere handful, and even they are mostly pessimistic about the future of dolphins.

"They will be exterminated because of our doings," postulates Dr. van Heel. "Consider our maltreatment of the sea or our catching industries that will go on catching until there is nothing left to catch and nothing left for the dolphin to eat. We are spoiling the sea at such a pace, the dolphin will be out before we get in!"

I not only share this doom-ridden forecast but believe the danger is more comprehensive than the purely physical dangers of man's unthinking assault on the sea.

My fears are concerned with our basic attitudes, and the following illustrates this more poignantly than any other example. It also bears dramatically on the beliefs, complacent beliefs in my opinion, of those optimists who see hope for dolphins in the new wave of ecological awareness that has arisen in the last decade. We cannot assume, as I think this next story shows, that the ecology wave will reach down far enough, quickly enough, to save the dolphin.

Some time ago a leading record company, Capitol, produced a disc that at first glance appeared to contradict the ferocious commercial dictates of such companies. This was no superbeat group or teenage idol but a collection of songs recorded underwater from humpback whales! It is a piece of sound magic, music from another universe, the communications of our first alien species.

Dr. Roger Payne, who recorded the "singing" whales, is now one of my committed respectful scientists, and when I first heard of this record, or more specifically, of the fact that it had been, as Capitol forecast, a great success, I felt that there really was hope for the cetaceans. If the general public could sit and listen with respect, then perhaps the denigration I gloomily saw had been partially evaporated by the ecological lobby.

It was only when I read of Dr. Payne's underlying personal motive for studying whales that I realized that the disc was evidence of the opposite—a bizarre vindication of my own fears. What we have here is a commercial disc being listened to with wonder and delight by a huge public audience—produced by a scientist who is appalled at what that same public will do to animals, even animals now widely recognized as sensitive and intelligent. Dr. Payne explains how it all began when he went to see a dolphin that had been washed up on an American beach:

> It was a small whale, a porpoise about eight feet long with lovely subtle curves glistening in the cold rain.

It had been mutilated.

Someone had hacked off its flukes for a souvenir. Two other people had carved their initials deeply into its side and someone else had stuck a cigar butt in its blowhole.

Although it is more typical than not of what happens to whales when they encounter man, that experience was somehow the last straw and I decided to use the first possible opportunity to learn enough about whales so that I might have some effect on their fate.

There are more "straws" than that. They are grisly and will turn your stomach. But having spent most of this book putting the dolphin in his rightful place I hope now, with what will follow, to reach out to that souvenir hunter and the initial carvers, and the person who used a dolphin for an ashtray, and present *them* with a few final straws.

We have got to stop abusing, mutilating, denigrating dolphins in the interests of our own mental health. In the same way as the South African nation will be a sick nation as long as it practices racism and bends truth and humanity to justify fear, so the human race as a group will never be anything more than a primitive animal as long as it abuses anything it regards as alien. The dolphin is a test not just of our intelligence but of our awareness, our courage and our humanity.

At the moment I wonder whether we even have a right to apply the word "humanity" to the human race.

Pilleri and Brenner of the Brain Anatomy Institute of Berne, Switzerland, paused recently from their complex studies of cetacean neurology to indulge in an emotional outburst aimed at a wide audience. These two staid scientists were angry, as can be gathered from the title of their piece—"Man—the Butcher of the Seas from Fifty Millions to Fifty"—and they wrote with no punches pulled.

Recording that whales had conquered the hostile environment of the sea "long before the first creature resembling a human being inhabited the earth," the authors went on to consider the "dramatic confrontation" that was to occur fifty million years later with man.

"Out of his helplessness and feebleness Man developed a

weapon that gave him power over all the Earth: His Brain." Pilleri and Brenner described this as "Intelligence that became the tool of his thirst for absolute power."

"Whereas Nature required fifty million years to develop a form of life which not only survived in an element hostile to its kind but established itself firmly in that element, it has taken Man only fifty years to bring that same form of life to the brink of extinction."

Whale slaughter, they point out, goes on today in spite of the International Whaling Commission strictures. There was a reduction in licensed killing for 1975–76 of five thousand whales. What does this mean when the licensed total exceeded thirty thousand? And who knows how many unlicensed whales are killed?

The Swiss scientists also reveal an interesting statistic relating to the "point" of the whaling industry. Nobody needs to eat whales. Even the Japanese, for whom whale meat has always been a regular item of diet, take only 1 percent of their daily 78.4 grams of protein from the whale meat they eat. And as Pilleri and Brenner point out, you only need 44 grams of protein a day for a healthy way of life.

There is no commercial point to the whale slaughter! What is more, the lobby against the slaughter of whales, in spite of the recent frantic spate of effort, best exemplified by the activities of Green Peace, is not winning. What is needed is a dramatic basic change of attitude toward the status of whales and man in the natural universe. There is no point, for example, in stopping the Russians from killing whales with harpoons and allowing them and other nations to convert their factory ships to processing plants for krill, the food of the whales.

What happens when the big whales are dead? Do we then, as Dr. van Heel suggests, "go on catching until there is nothing left to catch," right down the line to the small whales, the dolphins?

In fact, we are catching dolphins and eating them already. Or I should say certain people, in particular the Japanese, are catching dolphins and eating them. The Americans are catching dolphins and simply throwing the corpses away, and we will look at that in a moment. First I think you should hear how the Japanese catch their dolphin dinners.

In the Sea of Japan and into the Pacific, thousands of catching craft go out every year to hunt dolphins. They wait until the friendly animals appear around the boats, glide on the bow waves, or simply come in for a curious peep. A hinged, barbed harpoon answers this contact, and harpoon and rope are attached to a wooden float.

As the dolphin's skin is extraordinarily sensitive and the sensory areas of its brain are highly developed, the kind of suffering these animals must experience as they are towed for hours with the hinged barbs constantly tearing deeper into their bodies (the catcher boats do not stop until a "worthwhile" number of animals are in tow) is certainly beyond my ability, or desire, to imagine. But it doesn't end there. They are hauled on board by a fisherman using a hook on a pole; the hook is impaled into the dolphin's side, whereupon it is jerked on board to bleed to death if it has not already, and perhaps mercifully, died of shock and pain.

The cries these dying dolphins make as they are hauled through the bloody water provide the fishermen with another crowd of victims, as other dolphins home in on the distress cries of their harpooned fellows. And I have even heard of an incident where, for lack of a suitable catch, a live dolphin was taken from the water with a lifting hook, nailed to a board through its flippers and towed behind a boat until its cries attracted others of its species.

Is this all too far from home for you? Are the Japanese fishermen too remote a peasant species? Consider then a parable a good friend of mine wrote some years ago. He was out to make a point similar to the point of this book, and he sugarcoated it as science fiction. But as I am told 60 percent of Americans read their Bible every day, I think you might recognize the tale and see its relevance to dolphins dying nailed to boards and screaming to their fellows.

This story considered a meeting of the Inter-Galactic Council in session to consider new admissions. Had the Planet Earth, the Chairman asked, reached a point of development that would allow its inhabitants to be safely let loose among the other citizens of the Universe? The answer was no.

"The last observer we sent down," the Chairman is told, "they nailed to a wooden cross until he choked to death."

The Chairman is suitably shocked, but as arbitrator of so large an area, much of it extremely violent, he demands an expansion of that statement. "Did they appreciate who he was? Did they realize he was special? What's more to the point, have they learned from that lesson? It's a long time since that happened and it's not the first Observer we've lost."

Sadly the reporter sets the Chairman straight: "Rather than admit that they did it they have spent the last 2,000 years building a cult of justification which promotes the belief that the event actually saved the world."

Thus today, God is still in his Heaven and Jesus may have saved man from his own conscience but there is little hope for the other intelligent inhabitants of our planet. We follow the Old Testament edict: "So God created man in his own image, in the image of God created he him; male and female created he them. And God blessed them, and God said unto them, Be fruitful, and multiply, and replenish the Earth, and subdue it: and have dominion over the fish of the sea, and over the fowl of the air, and over every living thing that moveth upon the earth."

Do we really still believe that there is a godly justification for the statistics? Turkey kills thirty thousand dolphins a year officially, hunted by rifles from boats; Uruguay kills some two thousand a year; Japan keeps no record; in the Faroes they specialize in the totally pointless killing of innocent pilot whales until the harbors run red with blood; and in America there is a huge, unholy slaughter of dolphins now totaling millions!

Next to Japan, America is the biggest killer of dolphins in the world. America also has less justification for the dolphins it kills than Japan. They are the useless by-product of a luxury fish, tuna. These dead dolphins—kills have run as high as 200,000 a year in the past—are simply thrown away.

Before going into this American slaughter in more detail (I

am determined so to do because it is *the* most unjustified, criminal and pointless slaughter in the world), I want to relate an incident that I experienced in an American restaurant in 1977 and that throws some light on the public attitude.

I was shown a menu that offered "dolphin." I caused an incident. I am not by nature a demonstrator, but that one word brought on a flush of anger and revulsion that made me an instant agitator. Many of my American friends are bothered by what might be called the "food excess" that seems endemic in the U.S. Meat served in portions too large to be eaten or shrimp decorated with enough salad to feed a family is an obscene waste, but to offer dolphin in a country grossly overendowed with good food seemed somehow to be the ultimate manifestation of indifference.

So I staged my own individual demonstration. I inscribed "Eating Dolphins Is Obscene" on the large white table napkin and hung it over the edge of my stall for all the customers to see.

An extremely flustered waitress called an even more flustered manager, who in the nicest possible way asked me if I would remove my sign. I asked him how many people ate dolphin in his restaurant. He answered that it was one of the most popular fish dishes. Dolphins, I corrected him, were not fish, but mammals like us. He grinned with huge relief and explained that the dolphin on offer was not actually dolphin but dorado—an island term for the fish. How many of his customers, I asked, knew that? He wasn't sure. To draw an obvious conclusion, it wouldn't have made much difference to his customers if the dorado had been dolphin proper.

Which goes some way to explaining, I suggest, the extraordinary state of affairs that presently exists with dolphins and the tuna-fishing industry in America. Not enough Americans care!

I have taken my synopsis of this bizarre situation from the chronicles of the San Francisco–based Save the Dolphin group, who so far as I know have monitoring facilities which are as up to date as any.

Going back a few years, the American Senate decided that something had to be done about the hundreds of thousands of dolphins indiscriminately killed by the lucrative American tuna-fishing industry. Tuna fishermen use dolphins to find tuna. No one knows exactly how or why, but tuna swim where dolphins swim. The best explanations are a similarity of food targets, though others think the tuna use the dolphin's navigational ability. For the fishermen the shoals of dolphin who swim close to the surface are proof positive of tuna down below, and an entire fishing system has been based on this pattern. "Sets" of purse seines (nets with drawstrings) are cast around the dolphin shoal and when drawn up produce a fine catch of tuna—and dolphins! The dolphins die in the nets, they die when the nets are pulled in and they are killed by fishermen on the deck. These dead dolphins are cast back into the sea. Every time you open a can of tuna, you are in effect killing a dolphin!

The figures for these pointless deaths were never properly computed until the dolphin activists demanded action. But when it became known that perhaps a quarter of a million dolphins were being killed annually, that this slaughter had been going on for years and that one species, the spinner dolphin, had dropped to between 50 and 60 percent of original, the federal government acted and a bill was passed which set a quota for dolphin kills and a short-term objective—that dolphin kills be reduced to "insignificant levels approaching zero" by 1977.

For those concerned with dolphins the quota was extraordinarily high—78,000 for 1976!—but we live in a pragmatic world, and the tuna lobby made great play of the jobs that would be lost if any kind of real ban were imposed.

Since then the situation has grown even more farcical.

Scott Sinclair, a National Maritime Fisheries Service observer on a number of tuna boats that went out in 1976 to monitor the 78,000 quota, went into print last year with the opinion: "I personally feel that upwards of 125,000 perished during the year."

And this was the count of just one observer. There should, he suggested, be observers on every tuna boat; the very presence of the observer acts as a deterrent against illegal activities. It is completely illegal, under the federal legislation, to set nets around striped dolphins, for example. But Sinclair suggests that there would have been two such sets involving high mortality of striped dolphins had he not been on board a particular boat.

In a sense all of this is totally irrelevant. There is no justification for killing *any* dolphins, quite apart from 78,000 officially and God knows how many hundreds of thousands unofficially. Official policy accepts this, and the American public—no, the world public—should make it clear to their administrators that this slaughter is morally unacceptable.

It is equally unacceptable practically. Are we honestly being asked to believe that nations with the industrial and technological abilities of Japan and the United States of America cannot (a) find an alternative baiting/catching method for the tuna fleets or, if this is not possible (b) make it worth the while of the tiny tuna-fishing fleet to catch something else or just give up catching altogether and retrain to some other industry?

I regard the pathetic application of this law as another, and perhaps classic, example of the subliminal degradation of the dolphin species which underlies our general attitude, and it is this general attitude which needs to be altered if the dolphin is not to be rendered extinct.

If this seems radical and gives insufficient credit to the worthy efforts of groups like Save the Dolphin, I include it not to provide this book with some dramatic editorial theme but because I believe the problem is urgent. In terms of dolphin extinction, the time clock is approaching ten minutes to midnight, and the imperatives that are pushing that clock inexorably to its end are still endemic in the human community.

Let me give two good examples, one zoological, the other to do with our general thinking.

Dolphins will commit suicide under certain conditions of stress. They have never known our survival imperatives and if subjected to certain stress conditions, a wide and complex variety of conditions, they will quietly decide that life is simply not worth it.

As Bunnell puts it:

The Cetacean system appears to be a more integrated and contemplative one, evolved in conditions where immediate danger was not so likely as it was for most mammals. It is ironic that our technology, which developed as an adaptation to danger, has now presented the whales with dangers for which their own evolutionary history leaves them quite unprepared.

But just how unprepared? Cousteau and Lilly both record instances of dolphins quitting life under stress, and no great degrees of stress at that. When I heard that the spinner dolphin had been cut to 50 percent of its former population strength I was reminded, with alarm, of a situation which I saw in the Serengeti National Park in northern Tanzania. That park was once famous for its huge herds of zebra and wildebeest. Millions of these animals walked traditional migration routes across vast areas of country from what was Tanganyika through into Kenya.

Political and economic realities disrupted these vital traditional paths, the most dramatic being the growth of the city of Nairobi, the capital of Kenya. Visit the Nairobi National Park today and try to find any substantial number of zebra or wildebeest! If you move down into the 5,000 square miles of the Serengeti you will fare a little better, but only marginally. In terms of the herds that existed thirty years ago you will be photographing shadows.

It was realized far, far too late that zebra and wildebeest need the security of numbers to keep their normal breeding patterns operative. Reduce those numbers to a certain "break-even" point and some strange genetic trip switch cuts in. If a zebra herd reaches a small size it appears to stop breeding actively. It commits what amounts to a form of group suicide when its numbers reach a point where it cannot accommodate predation. The herd quits.

The question I wish to ask—and I can tell you now that no one knows the answer—is, Do the notoriously stress-sensitive dolphin shoals quit when their numbers are dramatically reduced? My justification for asking so apparently meaningless a question is this. It is not good enough to say there are still 50 percent of the Pacific spinner dolphins left when we have evidence from other animal species to indicate that gross reduction of numbers is the trip switch to the extinction of those left.

I would like to see the American "quota" reduced to zero now, because I suspect that the dolphin, a herd animal similar to the zebra, might not be in danger of just losing half its numbers, but of a group suicide that spells extinction. And I personally do not want to have to tell my children, or at best my grandchildren, that once there lived upon the earth an equal being with a brain as large as ours, with an intellectual sensitivity the equal of ours, which we slaughtered so that we might enjoy the limited delights of a tuna salad! If I am ever reduced to telling such a tale I think I would feel obliged to hide from my grandchildren. They, I suspect, would feel obliged to hide from me.

And now the example to do with our general thinking. Presented as dramatically as the situation above, the majority of thinking people would say that it could not happen.

But what will stop it? Legislation? A new ecological awareness? Books like this? I think not. The only thing that will stop it is a new set of basic parameters concerned with our essential status thinking about dolphins, and those parameters do not exist at the moment. Consider. . . .

A very large part of the new knowledge we have of dolphins has come from the investment by the military establishment. U.S. Navy scientists, of all people, know more about these animals than anyone, and among the ranks of these experts there is a genuine awareness, respect and no small degree of reverence.

Has this awareness, this respect, this wealth of knowledge, made one whit of difference to the status of the dolphin in the military context? I'm afraid not.

In the interests of this book, I obtained as comprehensive a collection of military research data as the classified limitations permit. I have all three Sealab official reports, running to some six hundred pages, weighing down my files. I have the "General Summary of the Navy's Marine Animal Program"—twenty-three pages, each page averaging ten short abstracts of Navy research programs, in some cases running years and the whole costing millions of dollars.

I have copies of everything that has ever been released on Operation Quickfind, involving the orca and pilot whale species of dolphin. And by pure chance I managed to obtain a thirty-page survey of data on Russian research in the dolphin field.

I have even taken the trouble to log anomalies to these official publications, such as the report which appears in Cousteau's book on dolphins in which he quite innocently reports that an animal called Dolly, which formed an unusual attachment to a Miami housewife, Jean Ashbury, was a reject from a U.S. Navy training establishment. Cousteau apparently did not realize that this establishment at Key West is not on the official list of Navy dolphin-research establishments. He does admittedly voice suspicions—"the base was known officially as a 'study center' since the Navy is reluctant to have it known that these animals are being trained for military service."

Which brings me back to my point. In spite of all that the Navy and all its committed researchers know about the dolphin, and may I again stress that they know more than anyone else, the dolphin is still only regarded as a useful weapon or at best a tool for man.

You will not find this stated in any of the official publications that you are able to read. In fact, you will find a lot of very sympathetic descriptions, in my opinion designed to lead you away from this reality.

My point is this. If the leading dolphin-research establishment in the world is prepared to use these animals as killers, and as expendable; to teach them methods which are completely foreign to their nature and in the final event to use them as weapon-carrying drones, what chance is there that the general public, who do not have their knowledge, can be expected to act with any greater compassion—the compassion that is needed to save the dolphin from extinction by the human race?

That concept, I accept, requires that I establish that dolphins have been used in this way by the Navy and I must confess that until very recently I despaired of ever getting anyone to admit that it had happened.

You may imagine, therefore, how delighted, not to say amazed, I was when I finally found an expert who was prepared to break silence on this issue. Perhaps I should not have been so surprised. David Taylor, the international veterinarian who has been featured elsewhere in this book, is very much his own man. Or to put it another way, dolphins need him rather more than he needs the people who tend them.

The fact remains that when I put to Taylor, who has attended many major international conferences and knows the American Navy researchers, what had become a traditional question—"Were dolphins used by the American Navy for offensive purposes?"—he answered squarely, "Yes."

And he was prepared to expand that statement.

Taylor has met and talked with veterinarians and civilian assistants to the Navy program who actually went to Vietnam with dolphins that had been trained for harbor-defense work. I asked just what harbor-defense work was.

"Dolphins were trained to carry a bayonet device on their beaks and attack enemy skin divers," Taylor reported. "They were definitely employed in an area which is pronounced something like Cam-Ran Bay—I don't know the exact location or spelling of the place.

"The system worked like this," he went on. "American frogmen wore an identification belt that gave out a continuous buzz that American dolphins were trained to identify—these training programs were all done Stateside."

At meetings and international conferences Taylor also picked up other items of information concerning military activities. Dolphins had been trained to identify different engine sounds underwater. They had been taught how to attach limpet mines and other devices. They had been trained to retrieve items from the bed of the ocean.

"I was of course warned," Taylor commented, "on one occasion by the most senior person on the program, that all of this was heavily classified, particularly the business of attacking humans underwater."

He mentioned a conversation which he believed confirmed by innuendo the other snatches of information he had overheard.

"A very senior official made this comment: 'You know, David, how many millions of dollars the Navy has poured into the dolphin-research program? Well, I can tell you, the Navy has got its money back and much more.'

"You only have to see some of their research facilities to realize that this was an accurate description," Taylor affirmed. "They even had complete operating theaters constructed entirely of copper in which complicated surgery involving sophisticated electronic equipment could be used."

Most of Taylor's information has recently been given public support in the U.S. On the *Tomorrow* show, Tom Snyder heard a former Navy research-program worker, Michael Greenwood, tell how dolphins were trained to take packages underwater and attach them to the bottom of ships and submarines. The Navy has released a film which shows a device called a "transphonemator" being used to control dolphins, to direct them in the accomplishment of a particular task.

With this direct, and in my opinion reliable, piece of reportage to work on it is possible to read between the lines of unclassified Navy material. It casts a new light on the apparent innocence of the friendly Tuffy diving to a buzzer operated underwater by the aquanauts manning Sealab. It projects an ominous alternative to the back packs designed and successfully carried by the pilot whale Morgan or the orca Ishmael, in the Deep Ops program. It takes no small shift of the imagination, and the Navy is patently not short of that, to replace Tuffy's conditioning to go to a buzzer with a similar program to attack those without a buzzer, or to replace the radio packs with an explosive device. I have no actual evidence that this happened but I would be very surprised if kamikaze dolphins had not been considered. The concept is within the framework of thinking about dolphins under which other, better-supported military activities have been conducted.

Consider these two items of information which appeared as recently as 1977 in a special issue of the influential and serious magazine *Oceans* dealing with cetaceans. In an article entitled "The Navy's Natural Divers," the author, Charles Barton, records that an Atlantic bottle-nosed dolphin, Simo, had been trained to butt sharks in order to ward off potential attacks on divers. Three paragraphs later he quotes Mr. Harris Stone, director of the Research and Development Plans Division, Office of the Chief of Naval Operations: "This idea that we have weaponized the animals to kill people is absolutely untrue."

My point is not to suggest that anyone is covering up; that is another issue. But if you take the fact that various Navy programs have taught dolphins

- to go to buzzers
- to carry devices in their mouths
- to attach devices to submerged objects
- to butt another species in an attack mode
- to differentiate between all manner of materials, including metals underwater

you end up with a serious credibility gap, and the Navy has no one but itself to blame. More important, in my opinion, you end up with an official attitude that the dolphin is nothing more than a tool that man has a right to use irrespective of that animal's personal interests.

Before leaving this subject let me stress that I am not pointing a particular finger at the U.S. Navy. I suspect that this detached, dehumanized attitude to dolphins is common to all countries with an interest in dolphins. How else could you interpret these comments, which I have already noted in other contexts, from a leading Russian researcher:

> The published data available give grounds for assuming that the dolphin's functional adaptation to life in the water, with special reference to the higher nervous activity, can, in principle, be put to use by man.
>
> . . . Because the animal is comparatively easy to tame and train, there is hope that it may be made to play the same role in the sea that the dog plays on land.
>
> . . . in studying the brain function . . . all the neurophysiological methods, from the gross one of brain extirpations and sections, to the fine up-to-date methods using microelectrodes, are essential.

And with that attitude existing among the experts we have no right to be surprised when a layman carves his initials in the side of a dead dolphin.

So where do we go from here? The government attitude is that killing 78,000 dolphins a year for the time being is okay. The official military attitudes rate them somewhere between tools and weapons, or dogs. The public sees no harm in desecrating their corpses, or eating what could be dolphin. And for at least one species, extinction might already be happening!

That is the situation we face in an age when a real understanding of dolphins—what they are, what they do, and, most important, the incredible things they may be able to do—has never been greater.

I am fairly certain that for the foreseeable future the dolphin needs to be protected from man, and this view is shared by many, perhaps most importantly by John Lilly. Two years ago he put his considerable reputation (his recent books have more than restored the dents inflicted a decade ago) once more on the line with an article in *Oceans* that caused a lot of people to think, "Lilly's at it again."

The article had the "crazy" title "The Rights of Cetaceans under Human Law." What Lilly was in fact at was what he's always been at—he was several years ahead of the rest of us in spotting the real danger to dolphins, and this was a perfectly serious article.

Lilly pounded all his old drums in this piece; he railed against "specicide," he respelled all his findings on the size of dolphin brains, he condemned man for his blind superiority complexes, he outlined the affectionate nature of dolphins and their capacity for fond parenthood, and then he ended it with a scary warning—scary for me, anyway, as one who has considerable respect for Lilly's prescience:

"We may already have accumulated too negative a reputation among cetaceans. Let us stop killing and enslaving them for our entertainment and our warfare. This we can do now."

And he announced that he was going back into serious dolphin research with this present worldwide threat to the cetaceans as his imperative; that he had formed a group called the Human/Dolphin Foundation which would have one primary objective—to communicate properly with dolphins.

Lilly explained: "We can, with dedicated efforts, communicate with them. If and when we break the communication barrier, then we and the cetaceans can work out our differences and our correspondences."

The program itself is exciting. Lilly will harness computers to his already vast store of information on dolphins and add to it via direct underwater contact with free animals. The "proposals" for the computer are in the course of preparation now. Someday, in the not too distant future, lightning-quick circuits may disentangle the kaleidoscope of images that are now known to be contained in the dolphin sound patterns and interpretation will be spun from that presently meaningless web. A loudspeaker will croak something that is meaningful to two groups of listeners—ourselves and the dolphins.

If only we could tell them to keep away until that moment!

Unfortunately, that is the final dolphin paradox—we need them to forge that first and vital communication, but we will denigrate them all the time they are in range.

In the meantime then, our only course is to broadcast an understanding of what dolphins really are to as wide a public as possible. Talk about them, take your children to see them.

If the dolphin is to survive until the moment of contact, we must educate our kind to realize that the dolphin is not a threat, be he our intellectual equal or physically superior. They may well be a sublime example for man.

I began this book with a loaded question from the poet-naturalist Robert Ardrey, and I will borrow another to pose my final point:

> Civilization lacks nothing in its imitation of Nature. What it lacks and lacks only is its recognition of man as an animal. What shall we do? How shall we proceed? Shall we make a man to fit the world, or a world to fit the man? It is an open question probably unanswerable.

It may be an open question, but it cannot be allowed to go unanswered; the entire future of the world as well as our race is dependent on our finding the right solution.

The dolphin, closer to us than any species in the natural universe, made the decision as to what needed to be reshaped exactly according to the choice Ardrey proposes. By reshaping themselves to fit their world instead of the world to fit them, as man is attempting to do, they have reached a state of grace that fits our concept of Utopia ahead of us. Their lack of aggression, intelligent interest, friendship for no reward and magnificent creative play are a reflection of Utopia that we may all recognize.

To destroy them may well be the same as killing the only angel that knows the way to heaven, and an overt recognition of this accounts for the inexplicable attraction—the lure—that the dolphin has for man.

TEN

Coda—the Dolphin Utopia

HERE, within this small scrap of cosmic detritus, we mammals of the sea both large and small have been graced with the major endowment. Consider. . . .

The surface of this planet measures 197 million square miles and of that 139 million square miles is covered with water. But wait—that is only one concept of our dimension, a limited anthropomorphic concept. To move with us you must learn to think in terms of space, not of distance.

For example. The average depths of our nine-tenths of the planetary area is 12,566 feet; in fact, were the bumpy sections of the land surface of earth—those parts you call mountains—smoothed flat so that the planet became a perfect sphere, the entire surface would be covered with water to a depth of 8,000 feet. Yes, there is that much water!

And we are not confined, as you were before this visit, to the thin film of living space that is the dry land. How high have you built, or how deep have you burrowed on the land? A few thousand feet at most! And to use these paltry intrusions into the sky or the land—to live there—you depend on machinery. You are like birds who may climb trees but cannot fly.

Our world—our living room, counting all of our head room, and side room, room before and room behind, the surfaces above and the depths below—is *331 million cubic miles!*

Beyond your comprehension, not at all! For lack of an example you place too much value on the imperatives bred in you by the need to fight for a corner of your restrictive surface land. Think instead of the dimensions of outer space—you have dipped an inquisitive paw into your ceiling as we have lifted an inquisitive beak into ours. Is it not the case that confronted with the awesome emptiness of space your territorial imperatives change? There is no enmity among your space men. Well, they, alone of your kind, have tasted the size of our natural habitat.

To understand what we are and why we are it is necessary to understand that we have not only been graced with most of the space but that that "most" is beyond exploration. There is no discovering an end to it, for there is no meaningful end to it. There is no need to guard one part of it, for one part is the same as another part. Example. We have been here some thirty million years and we have a facility for what you call memory which allows us to "remember" the elements of that time. Memory is habit ingrained in the mental structure of all beings, and you have noted with some wonder that one of our kind whom you term the pilot whale is given to grounding itself on the land for no known reasons. Only recently have your scientists noted that such groundings take place where once there was no land—where continents have moved and closed old sea passages.

Such theories have been labeled nonsense—how could any beast remember a passage closed for twenty million years? The answer, or at least one answer, is that memory is memory, that it is not shed like skin, and we have no knowledge that that passage had been closed. How could we have? When you have 331 million cubic miles to journey in, everything is new. Or more simply, if we were to take one year to explore 30 cubic miles of our world—no man could properly map that size of *cubic* area in so short a time—we would need ten million years to do the whole. The world moves a great deal in a time span of that magnitude. Which means there is no end to our journeys of exploration, for all would have changed by the time any were even partially completed.

And this affects us. The very essence of what we are, although we are aware that you have no great respect for the essence of what we are. We are not serious. We build nothing. Outside of ourselves we create nothing. Our brains expand for no good reason. We have no competitive spirit, or no spirit of the kind that you admire and instill in your young for the advancement of your species.

If you were to be presented with our world to live in, all that you are as a species now would die. You would become like us. You would not be joined as tribes, grouped as countries, separated by color, class or creed. All these imperatives stem from the smallness of your world.

Let us consider the possibility that one day one of your spacecraft discovers another world, as pleasant and temperate as this. The only difference is that it is bigger, shall we say a million times as large as Earth. If you were to take each of your present nations and place them in separate parts of this giant world, and to each of the units of these nations offer total freedom of expansion, what would happen?

Think before you answer, and consider the size we have mentioned. Between Africa and the United States the distance would be 6 billion miles; twice that between the U.S. and Asia, and these continents would have land areas equally enlarged. We think if you were to ever discover such a world it would be a honeypot trap for your species. It would puff out the frantic energies and claustrophobia that presently impel you.

We have never been so impelled; that is the essence of the difference between us.

Before taking this tour you were briefed on some of the aspects of us now established by your scientists. None of these findings has done a great deal to improve our status—we are still not serious, have built nothing and outside of ourselves have created nothing. And yet it is accepted that our brains have expanded to a larger size than yours. How can you resolve the paradox? Working only on the evidence in your possession, and we would stress that it is limited, it is surely possible to see something of our world through our eyes.

Let us begin with our body shape.

Our bodies are our buildings and our art. We have no criticism of our world. It is boundless, eternal, multifaceted, changing. But our original bodies were poor vehicles in which to move through this world. Now they are their own perfection. You will notice you feel no weight, none upon the body and none upon the mind. On the land you are constantly trapped and held and moved by a force you cannot see.

Although you are no longer aware that you are in water—what is water?—you can feel the perfection of movement from a perfect hydrodynamic shape. But what is shape? It is not a conscious structure but a device for movement, a device now so well made, so well adjusted to its purpose as to have no conscious effect. These bodies are sculptures expressing freedom, nothing else.

Movement—how may we describe movement to walkers? To birds perhaps, but even that comparison is primitive. There is no flapping of wings here. Movement is no more than a minute adjustment of lung breath, the gentle inclination of a fluke or the merest flicker of a tail muscle. We hang in our sky, are suspended in our world, not embattled by it.

And remember there are two worlds, worlds of different tactile sensation, a world to float in and another to breathe in. To understand you must imagine that your metabolism is that of the most bizarre alien—a vacuum breather. Think of yourself free of gravity, free to soar through your own sky, brushing mountains, swooping through canyons, playing tag with the clouds and hide-and-seek in the tops of trees—then gliding up and up when the time comes to sip a little of vacuum outside the atmosphere. We are sorry this is such a fantasy for you. It is the reality for us.

When there is a need for excited movement, then of course we can find speed! There are games to be played, the feel of the sea as it breaks up and over our storming tails, the skimming away of the streamlining molecules leaving drag and friction to dance their slow steps on our ghost skins. A roll in the sky, a spin in the air, a ride upon one of the bow waves of your boats, or a quick dash for food—all are games. There is a sophistication in play and the food hunt that perhaps you may never understand until you understand freedom.

But when we review the restrictions your world has laid upon you and the restrictions you lay upon yourself it is hard to see how you will ever come to understand this world of ours.

And if you cannot understand this world, which is the alpha and omega of our essence, the amalgam of our brains and our bodies, how will you understand us? The movements you see are, in us, sublimely easy. Our evolution, of the brain and of the shape, is a natural function of perfection.

There are, we must stress again, no practical limits to this freedom. Certain of our species have made a choice as to where they prefer to swim, but for all there is eternal change, unending room. We may go up or down, as and when we choose. Down as far as the desire takes us, the body closing in on itself, protecting itself from pressure; changing air into blood energy, then up, up (fast or slow as it suits), the body opening again. There are no threats from any of these other creatures in the sea. It is as if they have been put here in our service. Even the great shark, who is forced to swim in his narrow plane of pressure, can be moved on with a good prod from our hard beaks.

Everything else exists either to sustain or to delight us. You question why we have produced no works of art but do not question the further paradox that we have brains large enough to appreciate art. Could it be that there is enough beauty here, that the kaleidoscope is varied beyond comparison, that the hues of the sea, of the live scales of fish, of the rocks, sands and sea plants are their own canvas and that you may perhaps be limiting yourself by crediting the status of "artist" only to those who can interpret beauty and emotion to others? Would it not be true that if all your kind could make such interpretations there would be no need for artists? That you would all be artists?

An excuse? No, not in our case. But perhaps it would be if all we had to see with, as is almost true of your kind, were eyes.

Consider our eyes, our many different "eyes," and then consider us against any measure you would like to choose—as builders, say, or as artists, or as musicians.

For all of these are aspects of things you see and hear. Now consider what we can see and hear.

With our eyes we can see more than you—with our optical eyes, that is. We may see from beneath the sea; the beaten pewter of the surface, the black holes of the thermoclines, the shifting rays of an inquisitive sun, the dancing tricks of refraction, the gently shifting deserts of the sea bed, coral fantasies (busy builders these!) ranging across the architectural spectrum, the dark jungles of kelp alive with scaly things, slimy things, carapaced things, angel fish and devil fish, jellies and living rocks, undersea mountains painted with rainbow encrustations.

Yet with a blink, and a small adjustment of our optical eye muscles, we can see all that you can see. We may peer through the spume of storms, view sunsets and moonlight, dawns and cyclones; the towers you build along the edge of the world, the heaving buckets you float across our ceiling, the dark clumsy blobs, windowless (and we have assumed mindless in terms of their enjoyment of the sea), that you have lowered below the ceiling and that you call submarines. And we have seen you, and wondered. Oh how we have wondered! We wonder how you live, where you live, but most of all why you live. Do you ever really play?

But we must stress that these optical eyes, in spite of all they (in our terms) can see, are not rated particularly highly by us. There is even one of our kind that bothers with them not at all.

No, our true eyes are what you would call our ears, with some special connections and receiving equipment that as yet you do not possess. We may see a mirror view of converted sound, a view with depth, that sees inside and outside, around and about, measures and counts—with these eyes we may take a total count of all there is to be known within the ever-expanding balloon of the sonar mirror.

For example, friend dolphin swimming there—even if he were to remain silent, which, as you can hear, he is not—need tell me nothing. I know he is 100 feet away, swimming at 3 feet a second—see now he has just changed course, and is following the butterfish.

I cannot read his mind as such, but I can calculate his

thoughts by simply looking. You question that? His stomach is full and his lungs expanding and contracting under no great strain—so he has no need of the butterfish for food. In any event I can judge the speed of the butterfish and have "seen" that the rock it is now approaching has a large hole inside it; too small for friend dolphin. Now see, he spurts, it is a game. A boring game, I admit, for he can make the same calculations as can I. He can see the hole, judge the speed of the butterfish—it is just a moment's exercise.

Please believe that this example is trivial. To read all physical knowledge in a single sonar glance and to refresh that knowledge constantly with echo pulses, to know of the insides of things as well as the images presented by the outside, to be able to do all this by processes of millionths of seconds, is to have a comprehension beyond any example we can present for your kind. We are beyond conception in your sense, and I do not mean that in a derogatory way. All these processes, all this reading, all this seeing, are not taking place consciously. It is not like one of your radar operators sitting in front of a machine gathering special knowledge of a particular set of events for a specific purpose. We incorporate this special sense of seeing into our special state of normality.

And this is true of our sound communications as well.

In the sense that you have need of sounds, we have no *need* at all. Patronizing? No, objective. Consider friend dolphin again. I know everything he knows—his chances of success, his physical imperatives. I can assess the nature of his game be it food or fun and assess his chances of success. All this from a few clicks. What need of sounds that transmit information—what you call the spoken word—in that case? The only "voice" communication I need to make is one of appreciation—or scorn, or humor—all emotive sounds, all emotions that can be expressed other than by sound. Even your kind have developed gestures of the hands, expressions of the mouth, frowns, smiles, or at best a whistle of appreciation or a groan of contempt. To express an emotional reaction you need no sound, and we need them even less.

If that were the only purpose of communication we would be

completely silent animals. We are in fact very noisy. You must ask yourself why. No, you lack our ability to see enough in other ways to appreciate why you communicate as you do, by complex language. I will tell you why we communicate noisily. The primary purpose of communication is contact, an extension of the gregarious instinct that we both share. You confuse it with other things because you are obliged, with your limitations, to use communication for other, more basic, tasks. You pass essential information by sound and presume that it is the only way of passing essential information. You exchange images by sound and assume it is the only way of exchanging images.

But strip yourself for a moment of these needs. Conceive of a race of humankind that knows all there is to know of its physical universe, that has books enough to answer all the questions, computers so complex as to do all the equations and pictures upon its walls capable of every form of interpretation. Would humankind then cease to converse? It would not. We are gregarious animals.

Here this gregarious need is serviced by sound images so complex as to require that you amalgamate all your media to understand them. I will click ninety times in a second, and each click will be a ball of information that is comprehensive, subtle, definitive, humorous; tinged with warnings; warmed by emotional overtones; even a little aggression; and in the light of my sexual nature, of which you are aware, rich with innuendo.

Don't look puzzled, I am merely describing a concept of language which many of your own experts have described. Bernard Shaw spent much of his life attacking the limitations of your English language and proposing alternatives. Do you seriously propose humankind as a species that should be admired for its communicating ability when in this day and age there are possibly a thousand different languages and dialects? Or more to the point, in a world which admires its ability to communicate, and sees it as the factor which separates humankind from all other species, including ourselves, there is not one human being who can communicate with all other human beings.

You have had great difficulties communicating with us. This

has always been somewhat surprising in that, so far as we know, there has never been an instance where *we* have been anything other than interested in or desirous of communication.

In recent years we have become aware of the limitations of your vocal structure. Here, as you know, we use twice the sound spectrum that your limited auditory system can receive. I think we must both accept that until you have built equipment to compensate for these inadequacies, vocal communication will be very difficult. We could of course learn some of your limited sounds, and we will do our best. But the imperative, surely, must be on your side. We have lived by a code which allows an adaptation to new requirements, not a change of structures to them. Given time, a few million years, and a continuing human interest, no doubt we will adapt ourselves to speak within your sound ranges. If you want it any sooner, and I would again remind you that the limitations are on your side, you will have to supply yourself with another tool. It would be better surely if you changed yourself in the fullness of time to use our range, but we sense, as it would appear to be the nature of your species, that you will seek something more immediate even though it will not be as comprehensive.

As for the brain, well, we know nothing of the brain. It is an extension of all else. The brains we have are the brains we need. The brains you have are the brains you need.

We know something of your evolution on the land. Down the ages we have met your kind at different moments of its development. Again, that is not a criticism. There were no tigers in the sea. We were not so badly buffeted by Permian winds nor driven so close to extinction by the ice ages. No dinosaurs walked the bed of the sea. The sea has been our womb since we first chose it for what it offered. It was kinder then and it has been kinder since. So we understand the drives that have shaped your kind.

But you must understand that we are shaped by our world too. There is no danger here, so there is no fear. There is no hunger, so there is no justification for killing other than for the essential food requirement. There are no territorial limitations, so there are no territorial imperatives. There is no need for work, so motive comes from play. That we are gentle, forgiving, undemanding, inquisitive is not that we are special, it is simply the shape of our surroundings.

You say we have large brains. I say we have normal brains. No, that is not to say you have small brains. For your kind you have normal brains.

Why do we bother with you? We bother because evolution has no end. You are obsessed with "difference," determined that there should be a gulf. There is no longer any need. You have stopped building moats around your castles. You have even reached the point where you have a secret longing for communication with another species. Are your space probes looking for rock samples or life samples? Is this obsession with UFOs anything more than a rejection of cosmic loneliness? As I have said before, we are gregarious, and as you well know, we share a common evolutionary heritage. We are the same at heart, you of the land and we of the sea.

You will find your life on other planets when you have the technology to get there—the laws of logic and the size of the galaxy make that inevitable. The same goes for us. You will find us when you have the mental technology to recognize our existence, and if this visit, be it ethereal, is any guide, we are getting very close.

In the meantime, learn what you can of us, as we are interested to learn of you.

Appendices

APPENDIX 1. Herman Melville: *Moby-Dick* (Chapter 32: "Cetology")

. . . in some quarters it still remains a moot point whether a whale be a fish. In his System of Nature, A.D. 1776, Linnaeus declares, "I hereby separate the whales from the fish." But of my own knowledge, I know that down to the year 1850, sharks and shad, alewives and herring, against Linnaeus's express edict, were still found dividing the possession of the same seas with the Leviathan.

The grounds on which Linnaeus would fain have banished the whales from the waters, he states as follows: "On account of their warm bilocular heart, their lungs . . . "

Be it known that, waiving all argument, I take the good old fashioned ground that the whale is a fish, and call upon Holy Jonah to back me. . . .

. . . To be short, then, the whale is *a spouting fish with a horizontal tail*. . . .

To those who have not chanced specially to study the subject, it may possibly seem strange, that fishes not commonly exceeding four or five feet should be marshalled among WHALES—a word, which, in the popular sense, always conveys an idea of hugeness. But the creatures set down above as Duodecimos are infallibly whales, by the terms of my definition of what a whale is—i.e. a spouting fish, with a horizontal tail.

APPENDIX 2. EUTHERIANS (Placental Mammals)

Primitive insectivores, endentates (ground sloth, armadillo, anteater, glyptodon), primates (lemur, baboon, ape, early man), chiropterans (bat, flying fox), insectivores (mole, hedgehog, tenrec), rodents (beaver, squirrel), primitive creodonts, specialized creodonts, creodont carnivore stock (sabertooth, bear, wolf, lion, weasel), aquatic carnivores (seal, sea lion), cetaceans (zeuglodont—the archaic whale, baleen whale, sperm whale, dolphin), primitive ungulates, amblypods (coryphodon, donceras), condylarths, primitive even-toed ungulate stock, pigs (babirussa, wild boar, hippo), giant pigs (entelodon), ruminants (protoceras, syndyoceras, deer, *Sivatherium*, camel, giraffe, kudu, ox), primitive odd-toed ungulates (rhino, tapir, horse), proboscideans (maeritherium, palaeomastodon, tetrabelodon, *Elephas*), arsinoitheres, sirenians (dugong), primitive stock of South American ungulates, typotheres and astrapotheres, litopterns (*Macrauchenia*) and pyrotheres.

APPENDIX 3. Pliny the Younger (*Natural History*)

The swiftest of all animals, not only those of the seas, is the dolphin; it is swifter than a bird and darts faster than a javelin, and were not its mouth much below its snout, almost in the middle of its belly, not a single fish would escape its speed.

But nature's foresight contributes delay, because they cannot seize their prey except by turning over on their backs. This fact especially shows their speed; for when spurred by hunger they have chased a fleeing fish into the lowest depths and having held their breath too long, they shoot up like arrows from a bow in order to breathe again, and leap out of the water with such force that they often fly over a ship's sails. . . .

They are in retirement for thirty days about the rising of the Dog Star and hide themselves in an unknown manner, which is more surprising in that they cannot breathe underwater. They have a habit of sallying out onto the land for an unascertained reason, and they do not die at once after touching earth—in fact, they die much more quickly if the gullet is closed up. The dolphin's tongue, unlike the usual structure of aquatic animals, is mobile and is short and broad, not unlike a pig's tongue. For a voice they have a moan like that of a human being; their back is arched and their snout turned up, owing to which all of them in a surprising manner answer to the name of Snubnose and like it better than any other.

The dolphin is an animal that is not only friendly to mankind but is also a lover of music, and it can be charmed by singing in harmony, but particularly by the sound of a water organ.

It is not afraid of human beings as something strange to it, but comes to meet vessels at sea and sports and gambols around them, actually trying to race them and passing them even when under full sail.

In the reign of the late lamented Augustus a dolphin that had been brought into the Lucrine Lake fell marvellously in love with a certain boy, a poor man's son, who used to go from the Baiae district to school at Pozzuoli, because fairly often the lad, when loitering about the place at noon, called him to him by the name of Snubnose and coaxed him with bits of bread he had with him for the journey,—I should be ashamed to tell the story were it not that it had been written about by Maecenas and Fabianus and Flavius Alfius and many others—and when the boy called it at whatever time of day, although it was concealed in hiding, it used to fly to him out of the depths, eat out of his hand and let him mount on its back, sheathing, as it were, the prickles of its fin, and used to carry him when mounted right across the bay to Pozzuoli to school, bringing him back in similar manner for several years, until the boy died of disease, and then it used to keep coming sorrowfully and like a mourner to the customary place, and itself also expired, quite undoubtedly from longing.

APPENDIX 4. Pliny the Younger

Another dolphin in recent years at Hippo Diarrhytus on the coast of Africa similarly used to feed out of people's hands and allow itself to be stroked, and play with swimmers and carry them on its back. The Governor of Africa, Flavianus, smeared it all over with perfume, and the novelty of the scent apparently put it to sleep; it floated lifelessly about, holding aloof from human intercourse for some months as if it had been driven away by insult; but afterwards it returned and was an object of wonder as before.

The expense caused to their hosts by persons of official position who came to see it forced the people of Hippo to destroy it.

Before these occurrences a similar story is told about a boy in the city of Iasus, with whom a dolphin was observed for a long time to be in love, and while eagerly following him to the shore when he was going away, it grounded on the shore and expired. Alexander the Great made the boy head of the priesthood of Poseidon of Babylon, interpreting the dolphin's affection as a sign of the deity's favor.

Hegesidemus writes that in the same city of Iasus another boy also, named Hermias, while riding across the sea in the same manner lost his life in the waves of a sudden storm, but was brought back to the shore, and the dolphin, confessing itself the cause of his death, did not return to the sea and expired on dry land. Theophrastus records that exactly the same thing occurred at Naupactus too. Indeed there are unlimited instances.

APPENDIX 5. Pliny the Younger

In the region of Nismes in the province of Narbonne there is a *marsh* named Latera where dolphins catch fish in partnership with human fishermen. At a regular season a countless shoal of mullet rushes out of the narrow mouth of the marsh into the sea, after watching for the turn of the tide, which makes it impossible for nets to be spread across the channel; indeed the nets would be equally incapable of standing the mass of the weight even if the guile of the fish did not watch for the opportunity.

For a similar reason they make straight out into the deep water produced by the neighboring eddies and hasten to escape from the only place suitable for setting nets. When this is observed by the fishermen—and a crowd collects at the place, as they know the time, and even more for their keenness for this sport—and when the entire population from the shore shouts as loud as it can, calling for Snubnose for the denouement of the show, the dolphins quickly hear their wishes if a northerly breeze carries the shout out to sea. Their line of battle comes into view, and at once deploys in the place where they are to join battle; they bar the passage on the side of the sea and drive the scared mullet into the shallows.

Then the fishermen put their nets around them and lift them out of the water with forks. None the less, the pace of some mullets leaps over the obstacles; but these are caught by the dolphins, which are satisfied for the time being with merely having killed them, postponing a meal until victory is won.

The action is hotly contested and the dolphins, pressing on with great bravery, are delighted to be caught in the nets, and for fear that this in itself may hasten the enemy's flight, they glide out between the nets or swimming fishermen so gradually as not to open ways of escape; none of them try to get away by leaping out of the water, which otherwise they are very fond of doing, unless the nets are put below them.

When in this way the catch has been completed, they tear in pieces the fish that they have killed. But as they are aware that they have had too strenuous a task for only a single day's pay they wait there until the following day and are given a feed of bread mash dipped in wine, in addition to the fish.

APPENDIX 6. THE ORDER CETACEA

1. ODONTOCETI—Toothed whales including dolphins and porpoises:

PLATANISTIDAE
River Dolphins

PLATANISTA
P. gangetica
Ganges River Dolphin
P. indi
Indus River Dolphin

INIA
I. geoffrensis
Amazon River Dolphin

LIPOTES
L. vexillifer
Chinese Lake Dolphin

PONTOPORIA
P. blainvillei
La Plata Dolphin

ZIPHIDAE
Beaked Whales

MESOPLODON
M. bidens
North Sea Beaked Whale
M. layardi
Strap-toothed Whale
M. europaeus
Antillean Beaked Whale
M. mirus
True's Beaked Whale
M. grayi
Camperdown Whale
M. densirostris
Blainville's Beaked Whale
M. stejnegeri
Stejneger's Beaked Whale
M. ginkgodens
Japanese Beaked Whale
M. bowdoini
Andrew's Beaked Whale
M. carlhubbsi
Hubb's Beaked Whale
M. hectori
Hector's Beaked Whale
M. pacificus
Pacific Beaked Whale

ZIPHIUS
Z. cavirostris
Cuvier's Beaked Whale

BERARDIUS
B. arnouxi
Arnoux' Beaked Whale
B. bairdi
Baird's Beaked Whale

TASMACETUS
T. shepherdi
Tasmanian Beaked Whale

HYPEROODON
H. ampullatus
Northern Bottlenose Whale

H. planiforms
Southern Bottlenose Whale

PHYSETERIDAE
Sperm Whales

PHYSETER
P. catodon
Sperm Whale

KOGIA
K. breviceps/K. simus
Pygmy Sperm Whale

MONODONTIDAE
White Whales

DELPHINAPTERUS
D. leucas
Beluga Whale

MONODON
M. monoceros
Narwhal

STENIDAE
Dolphins

STENO
S. brerdanensis
Rough-toothed Dolphin

SOTALIA
S. fluviatilis
Bouto Dolphin

S. guianensis
Guiana River Dolphin

S. chinensis
Chinese White Dolphin

S. borneensis
Borneo White Dolphin

S. centiginosa
Speckled Dolphin

S. plumbea
Plumbeous Dolphin

S. teuszi
Cameroon Dolphin

S. brasiliensis
Rio de Janeiro Dolphin

STENELLA
S. coeruleoalba
Blue Dolphin

S. longirostris
Spinning Dolphin

S. dubia/S. graffmani
Narrow-snouted Dolphin

S. frontalis
Bridled Dolphin

PHOCOENIDAE
Porpoises

PHOCAENA
P. phocoena
Harbor Porpoise

P. dioptrica
Spectacled Porpoise

P. spinipinnis
Black Porpoise

NEOMERIS
N. phocaenoides
Black Finless Porpoise

PHOCAENOIDES
P. dalli
Dall's Porpoise

P. truei
True's Porpoise

DELPHINIDAE
Dolphins

DELPHINUS
D. delphis
Common Dolphin

GRAMPUS
G. griseus
Risso's Dolphin

TURSIOPS
T. truncatus/T. gilli
Bottlenose Dolphin

LAGENORHYNCHUS
L. obliquidens
White-sided Dolphin

L. albirostris
White-beaked Dolphin

L. obscuras
Dusky Dolphin

L. acutus
White-sided Dolphin

L. thicolea
Falkland Island Dolphin

L. cruciger
Hour-glass Dolphin

LAGENODELPHIS
L. hosei
Sarawak Dolphin

FERESA
F. attenuata
Pygmy Killer Whale

CEPHALORHYNCUS
C. commersoni
Commerson's Dolphin

C. hectori
Hector's Dolphin

C. heavisidei
Heaviside's Dolphin

C. eutropia
White-bellied Dolphin

ORCINUS
O. orca
Orca (Killer Whale)

PSEUDORCA
P. crassidens
False Killer Whale

ORCAELLA
O. brevirostris
Irrawaddy River Dolphin

GLOBICEPHALA
G. melaena
Pilot Whale

PEPONOCEPHALA
P. electra
Broad-beaked Dolphin

LISSODELPHIS
L. peroni borealis
Right Whale Dolphin

2. MYSTICETI—Whales with baleen food filters:

BALAENOPTERIDAE
Rorqual Whales

BALAENOPTERA
B. acutorostrata
Minke Whale

B. borealis
Sei Whale

B. edeni
Bryde's Whale

B. musculus
Blue Whale

B. physalus
Fin Whale

MEGAPTERA
M. novaeangliae
Humpback Whale

BALAENIDAE
Right Whales

BALAENA
B. mysticetus
Bowhead Whale

EUBALAENA
E. glacialis
Right Whale

CAPEREA
C. marginata
Pygmy Right Whale

ESCHRICHTIDAE
Gray Whales

ESCHRICHTIUS
E. gibbosus
Gray Whale

Reference Note

This book has concerned itself primarily with the interrelationship of the Dolphin species and the Human race and a substantial part of my material has been refined from lengthy debate with experts in many fields on the meaning, and more important, the relevance of the many things we have discovered about the cetaceans. Unless otherwise referenced, quotes are from these sources and from personal interview.

No comprehensive bibliography of scientific content has been attempted for purely practical reasons—the works of leaders in the field alone such as Lilly, van Heel, Norris, Morgane and Pilleri would fill an index many times the length of this volume. Instead, the work of these scientists, where related to my theme, are mentioned in the text and listed in the index.

Any conclusions drawn from these findings, or from comment in interviews, are my own.

Selected Bibliographic Notes

Fritz Khan, Gerhard Heberer and Herbert Wendt from Wendt's "Before the Deluge" (Victor Gollancz. London 1968/ Paladin 1970.) Aristotle/Historia Animalium Books One to Nine. Pliny/Natural History (Bostock and Riley. London 1855). Robert Ardrey/The Territorial Imperative (Collins. London. 1967). Norman Douglas/Birds and Beasts of the Greek Anthology. (Chapman and Hall. London. 1928). Cousteau with Philippe Doile/Dolphins (Cassell London. 1974). Herman Melville/Moby-Dick (Harper and Row. New York.) Dr. John Cunningham Lilly/Primarily from Lilly on Dolphins—combining Man and Dolphins 1961 and The Mind of the Dolphin 1967 (Doubleday and Co. Inc.) and from papers supplied to author for reference. Lilly and Ashley Montagu/The Dolphin in History (William Andrews Clark Memorial Library 1963). Reports of the Sealab and Deep Ops Programs supplied by the United States Navy. R. F. Scott/Scott's Last Expedition (Beacon Press. Boston. 1967). Margaret Howe from Lilly's The Mind of the Dolphin, as above. Richard Neville/Play Power (Jonathan Cape. London. 1970) Sterling Bunnell from Mind in the Waters (Scribners. Sierra Club 1974). Pierre Boulle/Planet of the Apes (N.A.L.O.W.L. 1963). Richard Wade from his film for Dutch Television/Who's Training Who. Dr. William Dudock van Heel from various publications of the Dolphinarium Harderwijk journal "Aquatic Mammals." Dr. G. Pilleri, from publications of the Brain Anatomy Institute/Berne, Switzerland. Roger Payne from notes to his record of the Song of Humpback Whale. Harold Hobbs/Follow a Wild Dolphin (Souvenir Press. London. 1978). Metaphysics concepts from some of Dr. Lilly's writings for Simon and Schuster, New York. Dr. Jacob Bronowski/The Ascent of Man (B.B.C. 1973).

Index

AUTHOR, journalist, and documentary filmmaker Robin Brown grew up in Africa after his family emigrated overland from Britain. As a journalist, he specialized in the reporting of the changing politics of Africa and wrote two novels, *When the Woods Became the Trees* and *A Forest Is a Long Time Growing.* He also began to study and write about African wildlife and anthropology. He quit Central Africa after disagreeing with the politics of white Rhodesia and returned to Britain to work in film and journalism. Responsible for some thirty network documentary films, his recent work has again focused on zoology and anthropology, with films like "The Animal War" on the conservation of game in Africa and "The Lure of Dolphins," which was shown on American educational television. Some of the early concepts now enlarged in this book were first explored in the dolphin film. Robin Brown lives in London and is now working on an international network documentary on "killer whales," orcinus Orca.

Photo: Ion Voyantzis